Kawanakajima 1553–64

Samurai power struggle

OSPREY
PUBLISHING

Kawanakajima 1553–64

Samurai power struggle

Stephen Turnbull · Illustrated by Wayne Reynolds

Series editor Lee Johnson · Consultant editor David G Chandler

First published in Great Britain in 2003 by Osprey Publishing, Elms Court,
Chapel Way, Botley, Oxford OX2 9LP, United Kingdom.
Email: info@ospreypublishing.com

A CIP catalogue record for this book is available from the British Library

ISBN 1 84176 562 7

Editor: Lee Johnson
Design: the Black Spot
Index by David Worthington
Maps by The Map Studio
3D bird's-eye views by John Plumer
Battlescene artwork by Wayne Reynolds
Originated by The Electronic Page Company, Cwmbran, UK
Printed in China through World Print Ltd.

03 04 05 06 07   10 9 8 7 6 5 4 3 2 1

For a catalogue of all books published by Osprey Military
and Aviation please contact:

Osprey Direct UK, P.O. Box 140, Wellingborough,
Northants, NN8 2FA, UK
E-mail: info@ospreydirect.co.uk

Osprey Direct USA, c/o MBI Publishing, P.O. Box 1,
729 Prospect Ave, Osceola, WI 54020, USA
E-mail: info@ospreydirectusa.com

www.ospreypublishing.com

Dedication:

To my sister-in-law Ann Arrowsmith

Author's Note:

The present work is the first full and detailed account in
English of the remarkable struggles centred on
Kawanakajima between 1553 and 1564. It is based entirely
on Japanese source materials and uses first-hand
observation of the terrain. In this context I would like to
thank the curators of the Kawanakajima battlefield museum, the Nagano Prefectural Museum, the Matsushiro
Museum, the Takeda Museum at Erinji, the Tourist
Information Centres of Nagano, Yonezawa and Kofu and
the Royal Armouries, Leeds, for their kind co-operation with
my research. I would like to thank my daughter Kate for her
administrative support.

Artist's Note:

Readers may care to note that the original paintings from
which the colour plates in this book were prepared are
available for private sale. All reproduction copyright
whatsoever is retained by the Publishers. All enquiries
should be addressed to:

Wayne Reynolds
5 Kirkstall Mount,
Kirkstall
Leeds,
LS5 3DT
West Yorkshire
UK

The Publishers regret that they can enter into no
correspondence upon this matter.

Editor's Note:

The numbering/lettering used to identify the Takeda and
Uesugi units on the Bird's Eye Views is not strictly sequen-
tial as the precise location of all units at all points of the
battle cannot be determined with certainty. The units identified are those whose location can be determined with some
confidence. To aid identification the same number or letter
has been used for any given unit on all three Bird's Eye
Views.

KEY TO MILITARY SYMBOLS

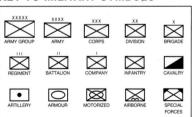

CONTENTS

INTRODUCTION   7
Background to the conflict

CHRONOLOGY   12

OPPOSING COMMANDERS   13

OPPOSING ARMIES   20

THE INVASION OF SHINANO   26

OPPOSING PLANS   34

THE STRUGGLE FOR   37
KAWANAKAJIMA
The first battle of Kawanakajima, 1553
The second battle of Kawanakajima, 1555
The third battle of Kawanakajima, 1557
The fourth battle of Kawanakajima, 1561
The fifth battle of Kawanakajima, 1564

AFTERMATH   87

THE BATTLEFIELD TODAY   92

FURTHER READING   94

INDEX   95

法性院大僧正信玄

INTRODUCTION

The romance of Kawanakajima

The story of the five battles of Kawanakajima, fought between the same armies in the same place over a period of 11 years, is one of the most cherished tales in Japanese military history, commemorated for centuries through epic literature, vivid woodblock prints and exciting movies.

The popular version of the story tells of a place deep in the heart of Japan's highest mountains where two rivers join to form a fertile plain called Kawanakajima ('the island within the river'). Here the two great samurai clans of Takeda and Uesugi fought each other five times on a battlefield that marked the border between their territories. Not only were the armies the same, the same commanders led them at each battle. They were the rival *daimyo* (warlords) Takeda Shingen and Uesugi Kenshin.

In addition to this intriguing notion of five battles on one battlefield, Kawanakajima has also become the epitome of Japanese chivalry and romance: the archetypal clash of samurai arms. At its most extreme this view even denies that there were any casualties at the Kawanakajima battles, which are seen only as a series of 'friendly fixtures' characterised by posturing and pomp. In this scenario the Kawanakajima conflicts may be dismissed as mock warfare or a game of chess played with real soldiers; an irrelevant but stirring tale of bloodless battles and gentle jousting.

I hope to destroy forever the myth that Kawanakajima involved nothing but mock battles. It is certainly true that in some of the encounters the two armies disengaged without the struggle becoming an all-out fight to the death. However, those casualties and wounds suffered were real enough.

With regard to the other aspects of the myth, there were indeed two great commanders. Each battle was fought between Takeda Shingen and Uesugi Kenshin, both individuals who loom large in Japanese history. There are strong veins of chivalry and romance, but these elements have to be seen in the context of some of the best-authenticated accounts of savagery in samurai history. In marked contrast to the tales of samurai glory, for example, the records of Kawanakajima contain strong evidence of cruelty to civilians; a topic otherwise hard to find in accounts of samurai warfare.

There is also the question of the authenticity of the remarkable notion of five battles fought on one battlefield. Unlike Japan's three battles of Uji in 1180, 1184 and 1221, which were fought on one battlefield because they were all contests for control of the Uji bridge, the battles of Kawanakajima did not have a single focussed objective. They were fought at five different locations within the Kawanakajima area called Fuse, Saigawa, Uenohara, Hachimanbara and Shiozaki. To complicate matters further, an examination of the list of battlefields generates more than five

OPPOSITE **Takeda Shingen depicted in a particularly fierce mode in a scroll in the Watanabe Museum, Tottori. He is usually shown wearing this helmet with a horsehair plume. Note also his Buddhist monk's *kesa* (scarf).**

battles! The battle of Fuse in 1553 is conventionally regarded as the first battle of Kawanakajima, but can only be understood in the context of the battles of Hachiman (of which there were two), fought just to the south of the Kawanakajima plain during the same year. The battle of Saigawa (the second battle of Kawanakajima) in 1555 was an indecisive standoff almost overshadowed by the nearby siege of Asahiyama. The third encounter, the battle of Uenohara in 1557, was fought further away from Kawanakajima than any other of the five and took place after the bitter siege of Katsurayama castle. The succession of events that included the fifth battle finished with another standoff when almost no fighting took place at all. It may even be possible to label another encounter in 1568 as the sixth battle of Kawanakajima. In fact only the fourth battle at Hachimanbara in 1561 was fought in the heart of Kawanakajima. This great battle overshadows the others as the culmination of the struggle, so that to many historians it is *the* 'Battle of Kawanakajima'. It is the fourth battle of Kawanakajima at Hachimanbara that is the main focus of this book.

Thus one could argue that there was in fact only one battle of Kawanakajima: equally by using a different counting system the number of separate engagements could be as high as eight. This is not quite the end of the matter, because if we define the battles by their general location in the Kawanakajima area and do not limit them to Takeda/Uesugi encounters, then the battles fought there in 1181, 1335 and 1399 should possibly be included, giving 11 battles of Kawanakajima – surely a world record!

I have taken the approach of viewing Kawanakajima 1553–64 as five separate but related campaigns fought over a period of 11 years against a common strategic background. The catalyst for the long struggle was Takeda Shingen's desire to conquer Shinano province. Kawanakajima lay practically on the border between Shinano and the province of Echigo. Echigo was the territory of Uesugi Kenshin, who was determined to stop his neighbour in his tracks.

Kawanakajima 1553–64 represents a transitional period in samurai warfare, and for this reason alone the five campaigns repay careful study. They encapsulate a shift from a time when firearms were scarce to an age when they were plentiful, and from an age when campaigns were cut short by the demands of agriculture to a time when virtually professional armies of samurai did nothing but fight.

Uesugi Kenshin is seen here in a very contemplative mood, as shown in a print by Yoshitoshi. Uesugi Kenshin's adoption of the life of a Buddhist monk was expressed in ways that stood in marked contrast to that of Shingen. Kenshin never married, and appears to have remained celibate all his life.

BACKGROUND TO THE CONFLICT

Japan in the Sengoku Period
The rivalry between the families of Takeda and Uesugi that found such memorable expression at Kawanakajima was in principle little different from many other conflicts that raged in various areas of Japan during the 16th century. This was Japan's *Sengoku Jidai* – the 'Age of Warring States' – an era of confusion and warfare that takes its name from the similar 'Warring States Period' of Ancient China.

Japan was no stranger to war, and the combatants of the Sengoku Period often looked back to the time of their ancestors to find parallels and precursors to their own deeds of heroism. Many of these folk memories were focussed on the Gempei War, the great 12th-century civil war, from which one clan, the Minamoto, had emerged victorious to seize the reins of government. The divine emperor was relegated to the status of a figurehead, and from 1192 real power in Japan was in the hands of the *Shogun*, the military dictator from the samurai class.

The power of the Shogun waxed and waned as centuries passed. The Minamoto dynasty of Shoguns lasted only three generations, and a doomed attempt at imperial restoration during the 14th century merely replaced the Minamoto's successors with another dynasty of Shoguns, the Ashikaga. The Ashikaga family proved much more successful at governing Japan, until a cataclysmic event in Japanese politics proved to be beyond even their control.

The great challenge came in 1467 when the Onin War, another fierce civil war, broke out. Much of the fighting took place within Kyoto, Japan's capital city, causing widespread damage to property and to the reputation of the Shogun. The spread of the fighting to the provinces proved yet more alarming, forcing the Shogun's provincial deputies to choose sides, and within a couple of decades the apparatus of central government seemed in tatters. The Shogun was openly defied in his capital, while beyond Kyoto the system of taxation upon which his government depended became increasingly meaningless. The powerful landowners or daimyo (literally 'great names') began to take control of their own affairs, as much for self-defence as self-interest. Some had once been provincial governors.

The battlefield of Kawanakajima looking across the plain from Saijosan. The modern city of Nagano lies in the distance. The Chikumagawa flows in the foreground.

CENTRAL JAPAN, 1542

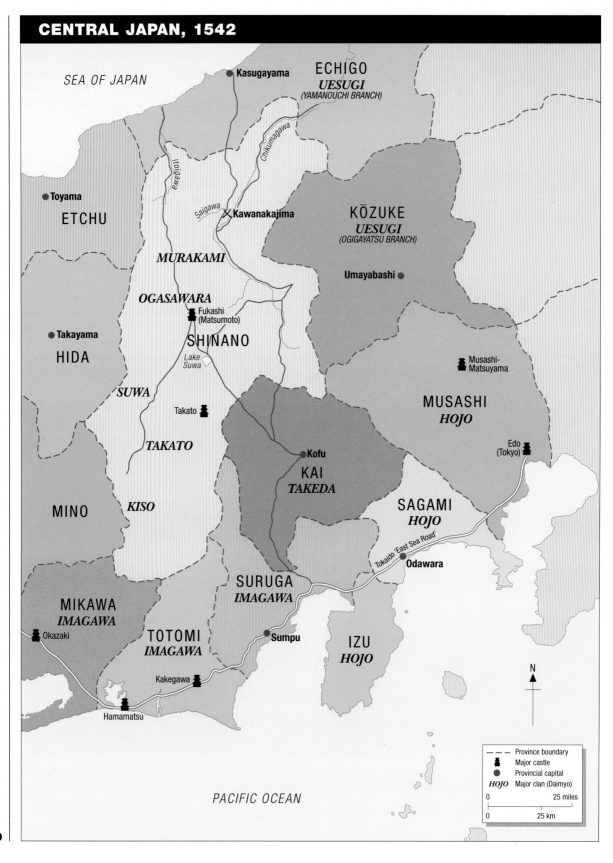

SEA OF JAPAN

ECHIGO
UESUGI
(YAMANOUCHI BRANCH)

● Kasugayama

● Toyama

ETCHU

Itoigawa

Saigawa

Chikumagawa

✕ Kawanakajima

KŌZUKE
UESUGI
(OGIGAYATSU BRANCH)

Umayabashi ●

MURAKAMI

OGASAWARA

🏯 Fukashi
(Matsumoto)

● Takayama

HIDA

SHINANO

Lake
Suwa

Musashi-
Matsuyama 🏯

SUWA

Takato 🏯

MUSASHI
HOJO

TAKATO

● Kofu

Edo
(Tokyo) 🏯

KAI
TAKEDA

MINO

KISO

SAGAMI
HOJO

Tokaido 'East Sea Road'

SURUGA
IMAGAWA

Odawara ●

MIKAWA
IMAGAWA

🏯 Okazaki

TOTOMI
IMAGAWA

● Sumpu

IZU
HOJO

Kakegawa 🏯

Hamamatsu 🏯

N

PACIFIC OCEAN

--- Province boundary
🏯 Major castle
● Provincial capital
HOJO Major clan (Daimyo)

0   25 miles
0   25 km

A mounted samurai of c. 1530, dressed in armour that would have been seen on the field of Kawanakajima. He carries a *naginata*, which was seen less often in a horseman's hands than a straight spear.

Some, like Takeda Shingen, hailed from ancient aristocratic families. Many, like Uesugi Kenshin, however, were highly skilled military opportunists. Such daimyo seized power through usurpation, murder, warfare or marriage – indeed by any means that would safeguard their positions and their livelihoods. This manifested itself in the form of *yamashiro* (mountain castles) atop hundreds of Japan's mountains. The daimyo used chains of these simple fortresses to control and guard their provinces from optimistic tax collectors and aggressive rivals.

The warlords of central Japan

In the centre of Japan's main island of Honshu lay the territories of some the most influential daimyo who fought each other in a bewildering array of alliances and rivalries during the first half of the 16th century. The Hojo family occupied the Kanto, the area around modern Tokyo. Beyond the Hakone mountains to the west along the Tokaido Road on the Pacific coast lay the lands of their rivals the Imagawa. Within the Imagawa territories the great Fujigawa (Fuji River) entered the sea. Upstream beyond the massive bulk of Mount Fuji was Takeda territory. This was the province of Kai (now Yamanashi Prefecture), which was mountainous and landlocked but had fertile soil and a long warrior tradition. North of Takeda-controlled Kai was the roof of Japan: Shinano province, also called Shinshu from the Chinese reading of the word.

During the early Sengoku Period Shinano province was not dominated by a single daimyo like Kai's Takeda. Instead a handful of minor lords such as Suwa, Ogasawara, Murakami and Takato farmed and defended their own jealously guarded lands. Shinano was also landlocked with just one province between it and the Sea of Japan. This was Echigo, corresponding to today's Niigata Prefecture. Echigo was ruled by the Uesugi, and was also home of the Nagao family, whose most famous son was to change his name to Uesugi when he took over their territories.

Takeda Shingen and Uesugi Kenshin fought each other in the area called Kawanakajima. It lay in the north of Shinano, the province that was the 'buffer state' between the two rivals.

CHRONOLOGY

1521: Birth of Takeda Shingen

1530: Birth of Uesugi Kenshin

1536: The siege of Umi no kuchi, Shingen's first experience of battle

1541: Shingen deposes his father when he discovers plans to disinherit him

1542: Shingen's invasion of Shinano begins with a move against the Suwa area

1547: The siege of Shiga and the battle of Odaihara allow Shingen to occupy more Shinano territory, and also illustrate his ruthlessness

1548: The battle of Uedahara provides a temporary setback when Shingen is defeated by Murakami Yoshikiyo

1553: With the fall of Katsurao castle Murakami Yoshikiyo flees to Echigo and joins Kenshin. The first battle of Kawanakajima is fought, consisting of a series of skirmishes at Hachiman and Fuse

1555: Shingen reinforces his castle at Asahiyama, which is then attacked by Kenshin. The second battle of Kawanakajima becomes a long stalemate across the Saigawa

1557: The bitter siege of Katsurayama opens hostilities for the third battle of Kawanakajima. An indecisive third battle is fought at Uenohara

1560: The battle of Okehazama destroys Imagawa Yoshimoto and elevates Oda Nobunaga, thus altering the balance of power

1561: Kenshin's siege of Odawara intimidates Shingen. The fourth battle of Kawanakajima

    25 September: Kenshin advances to Saijosan

    9 October: Shingen makes plans to surprise him

    16 October: Kenshin makes the first move and recrosses the river

    17 October: Kenshin surprises Shingen at Hachimanbara. A single combat is fought between Kenshin and Shingen. The detached Takeda force descend from Saijosan to save the day

1564: The fifth battle of Kawanakajima is fought at Shiozaki

1568: A notional 'sixth battle of Kawanakajima' takes place near Lake Nojiri. Oda Nobunaga deposes the Shogun Ashikaga Yoshiaki and occupies Kyoto, making the Takeda/Uesugi conflict largely irrelevant

1572: Shingen defeats Tokugawa Ieyasu at the battle of Mikata ga Hara

1573: The death of Takeda Shingen at Noda

1575: The Takeda are defeated at the battle of Nagashino

1577: Kenshin beats Oda Nobunaga at the battle of Tedorigawa

1578: Death of Uesugi Kenshin

OPPOSING COMMANDERS

No account of the Kawanakajima campaign or the events that led up to it can be separated from the personalities of the two commanders. The battles at Kawanakajima were essentially contests between two very powerful daimyo who ruled their provinces completely independently and paid respect, but little heed, to the nominal central government of the Shogun.

Takeda Shingen

The Takeda were an ancient samurai family descended from Minamoto Yoshimitsu (1056–1127), brother of the celebrated hero Minamoto Yoshiie. Yoshimitsu's son Yoshikiyo was the first to take the surname of Takeda. His grandson Takeda Nobuyoshi (1138–86) supported Minamoto Yoritomo, the leader of the Minamoto clan in the Gempei War of 1180–85 when the Minamoto fought the Taira. In 1192 the victorious Minamoto Yoritomo became the first Shogun of Japan, as a result of which the Takeda clan became very powerful in their part of Japan. When the Hojo supplanted the Minamoto Shoguns and were in turn replaced by the Ashikaga, the Takeda remained, officially recognised as governors of Kai province under the rule of the Shogun.

When the Onin War threatened the centralised government in 1467 the Takeda took advantage of the weakness of the Ashikaga Shoguns to establish themselves as landowners and rulers in their own right. The Takeda successfully made the transition from governors of Kai province to Feudal rulers without the need for a military coup. In 1519 Takeda Nobutora, born in 1493 and the current head of the family, established himself as daimyo of Kai in his capital of Fuchu (now the city of Kofu).

Shingen's territory of Kai lay to the north of Mount Fuji. Here we see Mount Fuji looking south from the province of Kai.

Nobutora proved a formidable leader of samurai, maintaining a fierce rivalry with his neighbours in general and the landowners of Shinano in particular. However, Takeda Nobutora is best known as the father of the famous Takeda Harunobu Shingen, born in 1521. 'Shingen' was in fact the Buddhist name Harunobu took on becoming a monk in 1551. This practice was by no means uncommon among the daimyo: Shingen's rival, Kenshin, did the same, and in both cases it is by their Buddhist names that they are best known to history.

Takeda Harunobu received his baptism of fire as a samurai warrior in 1536 at the early age of 15. His father, Nobutora, attacked a certain Hiraga Genshin at Hiraga's fortress of Umi (or Un) no kuchi, a few miles across the Shinano border. This was one of the Takeda clan's first advances into Shinano through the area known as Saku, a road that would eventually lead to Kawanakajima. Takeda Nobutora attacked Umi no kuchi with 8,000 troops, but was forced to retreat by a heavy fall of snow. The historian and poet Rai San'yo continues the story: *Harunobu asked to take up the rear. Nobutora laughed and said, 'You want to take up the rear because you know the enemy will not tail us. Nobushige would never do such a thing.'* Nobushige was Harunobu's younger brother and his father's favourite.

> *Harunobu insisted and took up the rear with 300 soldiers. When he was several miles behind the main body he stopped his men for a bivouac but warned them, 'Do not remove your armour. Do not take off your saddles. Feed your horses and have something to eat yourselves. We will be leaving at the Hour of the Hare. Just follow my lead.' His troops secretly laughed at him, saying, 'The wind and the snow are terrible. What is the point in doing this?'*

But Harunobu knew what he was doing. In the small hours of the morning he struck camp and marched his men back to Umi no kuchi in secret. They arrived there just before daybreak to find that Hiraga Genshin was so confident the Takeda had left for good that he had disbanded his army, leaving a garrison of only 100 men.

> *Harunobu divided his troops into three sections and personally led one section into the castle while the other two stayed outside with their banners flying, operating synchronously with those inside. The garrison of the castle could not work out the size of the enemy and surrendered without a fight. Harunobu cut off Genshin's head, returned with it and presented it to Nobutora. Nobutora's men were very surprised, but Nobutora would not give him a single word of praise, saying, 'It was cowardly of you to abandon the castle' In private his generals admired Harunobu, but they did not dare praise his achievements.*

Nobutora's animosity towards his eldest son continued in spite of the success at Umi no kuchi. In

The statue of Takeda Shingen outside the railway station at Kofu presents him as the classic Sengoku daimyo. He was skilled in war, a very good administrator, a skilled politician and a cultivated patron of the arts.

Here we see a view of Mount Fuji from Lake Suwa, with Takeda Shingen in the foreground. The Lake Suwa area was Shingen's first target in Shinano province. His red *jinbaori* (surcoat) appears on most illustrations of Shingen.

1541 matters came to a head when Nobutora resolved to disinherit Harunobu and pass his territory on to his younger son Nobushige. The young Harunobu had made plans of his own, however. He had cultivated the support of the senior retainers of the Takeda in Kai province and built up a strong but largely secret alliance with Imagawa Yoshimoto of Suruga. According to the chronicle *Koyo Gunkan*, Takeda Nobutora was blissfully unaware of the deal that Harunobu had made behind his back. When Nobutora went to Imagawa Yoshimoto to seek his support, Yoshimoto had him arrested. On 7 July 1541 Takeda Harunobu deposed his father and took total control of Kai.

The Takeda retainers clearly approved of their young lord's coup, and rallied round when the daimyo of neighbouring Shinano hurried to take advantage of the expected dissension in the Takeda camp. Their armies made a deep penetration into Kai within five days of the coup, but Harunobu was ready for them:

> *In the sixth month Murakami Yoshikiyo, Suwa Yorishige the keeper of Suwa castle and Ogasawara Nagatoki the keeper of Fukashi castle joined forces to create an army of 10,000 men and moved into the attack. Harunobu, leaving his general Hara Kaga no kami to stay in defence, advanced in person with 6,000 men to Nirasaki castle to hold off the assault. He summoned a total of 5,000 farmers and merchants of Kaga and Fuchu and made each one carry a paper flag and march forward to the accompaniment of drums and battle cries. The enemy retreated and ran away.*

Takeda Shingen used 5,000 farmers and tradesmen to make his army appear almost twice the size it actually was. The victory he won on 12 July at Nirasaki, a place uncomfortably close to his capital at Kofu, was the last threat he faced within Kai itself. All his future battles would be fought in the provinces of other daimyo, particularly in Shinano.

Shingen's personal life

Takeda Shingen's personal life was as flamboyant as his military activities. He had two principal wives and three mistresses, but they were outnumbered by possibly 30 others with whom he was intimate in a less formal sense. Clearly bisexual, he had a long-lasting relationship with his renowned general Kosaka Danjo Masanobu. Shingen's first wife was from the Uesugi family, and Harunobu was matched with her at the age of 13. She died young, and was replaced by a second wife who came to exert a positive influence on her husband, transforming this provincial warlord into a cultivated man of letters who could hold his own in polite society. Shingen's women between them presented him with seven sons and five daughters of acknowledged paternity, all of whom he used for cementing alliances through marriage.

Several portraits of Shingen survive showing a solidly built, determined-looking man, portrayed in later life with elaborate side-whiskers. Legend tells us that after his head had been shaved and he had taken his Buddhist name, Shingen commanded a portrait be painted of him in the likeness of the god Fudo, 'the immovable one', saying, 'Even if our neighbours attack our lands after my death, if they see this picture of me they will be deterred from doing anything serious!'

Takeda Shingen also governed his province with great success. Despite his military might, his headquarters in his capital at Kofu, then called Fuchu, was not a castle. He ruled from a *yashiki* (mansion) called Tsutsujigasaki, the apparent weakness of its defences symbolising Shingen's confidence in his armies and his subjects to defend him.

Takeda Shingen undoubtedly enjoyed the trust and confidence of his subjects. He encouraged civil engineering projects such as taming the waters of rivers. His farmers were unlike many of their contemporaries who readily deserted one lord for another. Part of his secret was the way he treated his subjects. This was helped by Shingen's money economy. The farmers were allowed to pay tax in the form of two-thirds rice, one-third cash. This also allowed for monetary fines to take the place of the usual corporal punishment in cases of brawling and indiscipline. Shingen owed his wealth to the gold produced in his territory, some of which could be panned from the rivers, the rest being mined. Details of the gold mines' productivity were kept strictly confidential, but we know that when Tokugawa Ieyasu took over the Takeda territories in 1582 he ordered the striking of 300,000 gold coins from the reserves of precious metal his men found.

Shingen is an example of the classic Sengoku daimyo. He was skilled in war, a good administrator, skilled politician and cultivated patron of the arts. He was also utterly determined and completely ruthless, slaughtering rival samurai and burning villages with contemptuous detachment. Few enemies experienced this cold and total commitment to a personal goal more acutely than his greatest rival Uesugi Kenshin.

Uesugi Kenshin

Uesugi Kenshin lacked Takeda Shingen's long and distinguished pedigree. His social position, and even his name, owed everything to clever opportunism. There was indeed an ancient family of Uesugi who were descended from the Fujiwara, and by 1530, the year of Kenshin's birth, the line had split into two branches: the Ogigayatsu Uesugi and the Yamanouchi Uesugi. The most illustrious samurai to bear the family name, Uesugi Kenshin, had no hereditary connection with the ancient Uesugi and even 'Kenshin' was a Buddhist name adopted later in life.

The future Uesugi Kenshin was in fact the son of a certain Nagao Tamekage and bore the original name of Nagao Kagetora. The Nagao were retainers of the Yamanouchi branch of the Uesugi and had some military reputation. In 1536 Nagao Tamekage set out from Kasugayama castle to fight the Buddhist fanatics of the Ikko-ikki of Kaga province. At the battle of Sendanno he was defeated and killed along with many of his men, although other sources say he died shortly afterwards from an illness.

Tamekage left four sons, Harukage, Kageyasu, Kagefusa and Kagetora. Kagetora was the youngest of the four. On their father's death, Harukage became head of the family, but his health was poor and he showed little ability for government. His brothers were commendably loyal to him, however, as the whole family were to their Uesugi overlords. When young

A statue of Fudo in the Takeda Museum at the Erinji. Shingen often identified himself with this fierce-looking deity and commanded a portrait to be painted of himself as Fudo, saying, 'Even if our neighbours attack our lands after my death, if they see this picture of me they will be deterred from doing anything serious!'

The site of Shingen's *yashiki* (mansion) of Tsutsujigasaki is now the Takeda shrine in Kofu city; the apparent weakness of its defences came to symbolise Shingen's confidence in his armies and his subjects to defend him.

Kagetora was 15, Harukage placed him in joint command of Tochio castle, along with Honjo Saneyori, where they were attacked by anti-Uesugi rebels but soundly defeated them. This early military experience earned young Kagetora a reputation akin to that of the young Shingen.

In 1545 Kagetora's Uesugi overlord called on his military skills again when a rebel called Kuroda Hidetada began a revolt at his castle of Kurotaki. One of Kagetora's brothers, Kageyasu, was killed in action and the young warrior marched off to seek revenge. The renowned young warrior's actions so alarmed Kuroda Hidetada that he begged for mercy. He was generously allowed to shave his head and become a monk, but during the following year of 1546 Hidetada went back on his pledges and again rebelled. Concerned at this rivalry among his retainers, the daimyo Uesugi Sadazane ordered Kagetora to attack Kurotaki castle and make an end of the Kuroda once and for all. The attack on a mountain castle complex standing over 900ft above sea level was rapid and completely successful, and Kuroda Hidetada committed suicide as his castle blazed around him.

It was clear that Kagetora was the strongest of the surviving Nagao sons and the best hope for the family's future. So, under pressure, Harukage was persuaded to retire, and Kagetora entered the castle of Kasugayama as his father's heir at the age of 19. He was now head of the family, but although all-powerful and respected around Kasugayama, Nagao Kagetora remained only a retainer of the Yamanouchi Uesugi to whom he had sworn allegiance. His masters had been in decline for many years, however, and it was inevitable that Kagetora should plan for the day when they finally relinquished power.

The Uesugi's main enemies had long been the Hojo clan, whom they fought for control of the Kanto, the area around modern Tokyo. In 1545, the year before Kenshin succeeded Harukage, the Uesugi had suffered their greatest defeat at the hands of the Hojo. The Ogigayatsu and Yamanouchi Uesugi branches had united to march against the Hojo's Kawagoe castle, defended by Hojo Ujiyasu's brother Tsunanari. With a garrison of only 3,000, Tsunanari managed to hold out against a supposed 85,000 besiegers. Hojo Ujiyasu marched to Kawagoe's relief with 8,000 soldiers and made a night attack on the Uesugi lines. His plans worked perfectly and Hojo control of the Kanto was dramatically confirmed by a crushing Uesugi defeat.

The reversal at Kawagoe was a calamity for both branches of the Uesugi, and while the fortunes of their retainers the Nagao prospered, those of the defeated Yamanouchi Uesugi leader Norimasa went from bad to worse. Eventually, defeated once again by Hojo Ujiyasu in 1551, he was forced to seek refuge with his followers. The obvious place to retreat to was Kasugayama, the castle of his leading vassal Nagao Kagetora. When Uesugi came to him on bended knee Kagetora agreed to protect his former overlord on his own very strict terms. Uesugi Norimasa must adopt him as his heir, give him the name of Uesugi and the titles of Echigo-no-kami (Lord of Echigo) and make him Kanto Kanrei (Shogun's Deputy for the Kanto area). Norimasa had little choice but to accept, so Nagao Kagetora was transformed into Uesugi Kagetora, the Shogun's 'champion' for the Kanto against the Hojo. In the following year, 1552, Kagetora shaved his head and took the name of Uesugi Kenshin.

Uesugi Kenshin's personal life

Uesugi Kenshin adopted the life of a Buddhist monk and his lifestyle stood in marked contrast to that of Shingen. Kenshin never married, and appears to have remained celibate all his life. As a result he never produced a son, so in 1564 he adopted as his heir the seventh son of Hojo Ujiyasu, who was given the name of Kagetora, Kenshin's previous appellation. In another contrast with Shingen, Kenshin is conventionally seen primarily as a soldier rather than as an administrator. Rai San'yo's history reports the following conversation between Kenshin and Murakami Yoshikiyo:

He then asked Yoshikiyo, 'Tell me, how does Shingen employ his troops?' Yoshikiyo said, 'He keeps them on the move, allowing them neither to be on the march nor stay in one place for too long. Every battle of his is aimed at a final victory.' 'He aims for a final victory,' said Kenshin, 'because his true desire is to cultivate the land. I am different. I meet an enemy and I fight him. I try not to allow my spear to be blunted.'

In fact, as the Kawanakajima campaign was to show, there was little to choose between Kenshin and Shingen in generalship, and both seemed to have enjoyed the confidence of their followers in matters of government. Something of the chivalry with which the two generals treated each other is revealed by another episode in Rai San'yo's history.

Shingen's province did not have any coastline. He obtained salt from the Eastern Sea [i.e. the Pacific Ocean]. *[Imagawa] Ujizane conspired with Hojo Ujiyasu and secretly closed the supply routes for salt. Kai suffered greatly. When Kenshin heard this he sent a letter to Shingen and said, 'I hear that Ujiyasu and Ujizane are using salt to torment you. This is cowardly and unjust. I fight you with bows and arrows, not with rice and salt, so I beg you henceforth to obtain salt from my lands.'*

OPPOSING ARMIES

The principal role of any daimyo of the civil war period was as a war leader, and their armies were efficient and well organised. Takeda Shingen and Uesugi Kenshin methods illustrate the system of delegation of command to a core of trusted relatives and close retainers. Takeda Shingen depended upon a group of senior officers popularly known as the 'Twenty-Four Generals', although the names of the officers that appear in chronicles and pictures vary. Some of them were Shingen's relatives, including three brothers.

Uesugi Kenshin had a similar band known popularly as the 'Seventeen Generals' or the 'Twenty-Eight Generals', depending upon which generals a particular artist has chosen to include. Among them were members of Kenshin's own Nagao family and allies such as Murakami Yoshikiyo who were treated on equal terms with the family.

Several others were to make names for themselves at Kawanakajima. One was Kojima Yataro, nicknamed 'the ogre'. He was over six feet tall, making him a giant among contemporary samurai. Yataro is famous for an incident during one of the Kawanakajima encounters when he was sent as a messenger to the Takeda. Shingen, showing an unusual contempt for the ambassadorial role, set a dog on him. Unperturbed, Yataro seized the dog and calmly delivered his message. When Shingen had made his response Yataro killed the dog with his bare hands.

The Takeda warband

In one section of *Koyo Gunkan* the entire Takeda army of 1573 is set out in some detail. Although this is a decade later than Kawanakajima, there would have been little difference in the overall organisation and the number of men supplied by the various named samurai, some of whom

The Chikumagawa, looking eastwards towards Hachimanbara and the city of Matsushiro.

Takeda Shingen depended particularly upon a group of senior officers popularly known as the 'Twenty-Four Generals', although different names appear at different times in chronicles and on pictures. This version is a hanging scroll in the Nagashino Castle Preservation Hall.

were the sons of generals killed at Kawanakajima. As social ties were very important in contemporary Japan it is not surprising to see an emphasis on the closeness of the relationship between the named samurai and Shingen himself.

The Takeda army consisted of three overall parts: the *sakikata-shu*, the *kuni-shu* and the *jikishindan*. The sakikata-shu was drawn from the former retainers of defeated enemies who had ended up as unemployed *ronin* (masterless samurai) and had joined the Takeda. The Sanada of Shinano are a prime example of how such men could provide loyal and valuable service. The kuni-shu (provincial corps) consisted of troops provided from the fields and villages by retainers. They included some poor samurai who were part-time farmers.

The jikishidan (the 'close retainer' group) was subdivided into four sections. The first was the *goshinrui-shu* ('honourable family members'). The second group was the *go fudai karo-shu*, the hereditary vassals of the Takeda and the clan's chief retainers. The third section was the group known as *ashigaru taisho*: generals of ashigaru (footsoldier) units. In spite of the traditional pre-eminence given to mounted samurai, the ashigaru and their generals were respected for their vital contribution on the battlefield. The jikishindan was completed by the *hatamoto shoyakunin* (personal attendants on the lord). Takeda Shingen had a retine of 884 men including various notable samurai as bodyguards, ashigaru and servants. Their numbers included administrative staff, Buddhist priests, elite messengers who used a centipede design on their flags, senior samurai advisers and young men whose title translates best as 'page'. These were almost invariably the sons of the elite samurai, and many of the Takeda Twenty-Four Generals began their military life as pages to their lord.

The most important fighting troops were the mounted samurai. The total number of horsemen in the Takeda army in the *Koyo Gunkan* list is 9,121. Every horseman would have been accompanied by two followers on foot giving a total Takeda army of 33,736, as follows:

Horsemen	9,121
Followers accompanying on foot	18,242
Ashigaru in the hatamoto shoyakunin	884
Other ashigaru	5,489
Total	*33,736*

The Uesugi warband

We see a very similar arrangement and system of classification among Uesugi Kenshin's army, for which there are two main sources. The first is the *On tachi no shidai* ('order of honourable swords') of 1559. There is also the very detailed *Go gunyaku cho* ('honourable service register') of 1575. Like the Takeda document, this is much later than Kawanakajima. The terms used for the subdivisions are slightly different from the Takeda, but there is a similar emphasis on the primacy of family ties. The first group is the *jikitachi no shu*. These are family members. The second category is the *hirotachi no shu*, consisting of the *fudai* (inner) and *tozama* (outer) retainers such as Nakajo Fujisuke and Honjo Shigenaga. The remaining group was known simply as the *samurai-shu*. There is no sakikata-shu. Up to this time the Uesugi kuni-shu had been regarded as separate entities, but from 1559 onwards they were fully integrated into the Uesugi army as retainers under Kenshin's command. Just as with the Takeda, the men's own followers would augment their numbers, and Uesugi Kenshin would also have had numerous personal attendants. The analysis of the fourth battle of Kawanakajima will show how both these lists translate into an army on the battlefield.

The mounted samurai at Kawanakajima

Prior to the Onin War the samurai had been regarded as mounted archers, but from the 14th century onwards many generals had given bows to the footsoldiers. This practice of using foot soldiers as missile troops eventually resulted in the most important change in cavalry tactics in the whole of samurai history. Samurai horsemen had to hit back, and needed to use their mobility and the striking power of a charge against missile-armed footsoldiers. So the bow was abandoned in favour of the spear as the mounted samurai's primary weapon. This development was largely complete by the time of Kawanakajima.

A re-enactment of Shingen's departure ceremony takes place annually at Kofu. The actor playing Takeda Shingen is pointing with his war fan, while around him sit his Twenty-Four Generals.

Takeda Shingen is customarily credited as the finest leader of mounted samurai in Sengoku Japan. At Uedahara in 1548 and at Mikata ga Hara in 1572 the Takeda cavalry rode down disorganised infantry missile units, but it is important to note that Shingen's army was never completely mounted. Even though the most common expression for the Takeda army is *kiba gundan* (mounted warband), in reality it was always a mixture of cavalry and infantry.

The classic cavalry charge used the technique called *norikuzushi* or *atenori* (literally 'hit and run'), where horsemen and infantry on foot charged into the ranks of missile troops and broke them in one go. This would be followed by the technique of *norikiri* when a group of five to ten horsemen rode suddenly and deeply into the mass of the disorganised enemy, throwing them into confusion.

Yamashiro warfare

Uesugi Kenshin was in no way inferior to Takeda Shingen in his mounted arm, and may well have been superior in his handling of infantry. The main disadvantage to possessing a renowned cavalry arm, however, was that the military situation in the Sengoku Period allowed daimyo precious few opportunities to exercise this superiority. The story of the Kawanakajima campaigns is no exception; Shingen and Kenshin spent as much time besieging castles as they did fighting field battles. The yamashiro (mountain castle) was a vital feature of warfare at the time of Kawanakajima, and the accounts of the five battles involve a great deal of activity around castles. Takeda Shingen may have boasted that his people, rather than the mansion of Tsutsujigasaki were his castle and moat, but away from his capital he depended as much as other daimyo did on a chain of defensive castles.

The ornate and beautiful tower keeps of surviving Japanese castles such as Himeji or Matsumoto did not make their appearance until the 1570s, however. The typical yamashiro of 1550 would have been a much simpler construction based around a series of interconnecting wooded hills. Straightforward wooden stockades linked towers and gates and followed the natural contours of the mountains. Using a daimyo's formidable manpower resources a technique developed whereby the mountain on which the yamashiro stood was literally cut to shape and adjacent hills sculpted into a series of interlocking baileys on flat horizontal surfaces, each overlooked by the one above it. On top of this framework were placed fences, towers, stables, storehouses, walkways, bridges and gates. Very little stone was used in the construction except for strengthening the bases of gatehouses and towers and to combat soil erosion from the excavated slopes.

Kawanakajima and the infantry revolution

The picture of samurai warfare in transition that Kawanakajima presents is reflected in the weapons and costume of both samurai and ashigaru. The most important development was in the use of firearms, which were almost exclusively ashigaru weapons. At Uedahara in 1548 the only

The Takeda cavalry in action, from the life-sized display at the Ise Sengoku Jidai Village. Samurai horsemen used their mobility and striking power to provide the shock of a charge against missile-using foot-soldiers. So the bow was abandoned in favour of the spear, and the mounted archer gave way to the mounted spearman. This development was largely complete by the time of Kawanakajima.

An alternative version of the famous Takeda 'Son Zi' flag, shown here being held by a samurai on a painted scroll in the Watanabe Museum, Tottori.

firearms seen on the battlefield were primitive Chinese handguns, but by the time of the second battle of Kawanakajima in 1555 Takeda Shingen owned enough Portuguese-style arquebuses to send 300 to Asahiyama castle.

Although a very primitive weapon to modern eyes, the arquebus had a revolutionary impact on Japanese warfare from the time of its first appearance in Japan in 1543. The most effective use of arquebuses involved rotating volley fire, but this was not properly developed until after Kawanakajima. Instead the Takeda and Uesugi arquebus troops were used in mixed units, and the main volleys fired by ashigaru were arrows. Kawanakajima therefore reflects a period when the potential of guns was still being realised.

By the time of Kawanakajima, close formation fighting by the ashigaru was becoming the norm. Their principal edged weapon was the *nagaeyari*, a spear with a shaft up to 18ft long. Some historians translate nagaeyari as 'pike', but the traditions of Japanese warfare favoured a much looser formation than was adopted by the Swiss pikemen. No Japanese battlefield witnesses the slow and remorseless 'press of pike'. Instead the ashigaru in the defensive hedge waited for cavalry with their spears at their sides. When the enemy was driven back the defensive formation broke up for a vigorous pursuit. The spear blades came in several forms. Some had a cruciform shape, others a crescent moon-shaped side blade for dragging a samurai off his horse. Some ashigaru would still be issued with the older *naginata* (glaive), but as the curved blade involved long sweeping strokes its use was somewhat restricted in close-formation fighting.

There was no particular difference between the Uesugi and the Takeda in terms of samurai weapons. The *yari* (spear) first appeared as an infantry weapon during the 15th century, and within 100 years different varieties became the favoured weapons for both mounted samurai and foot soldiers. The samurai's yari would be no more than 12ft long and its straight blade made it particularly suitable for stabbing. A certain Hosokawa Yoriharu is noted in the 14th-century *Taiheiki* as being killed instantly on receiving a spear thrust to his throat, while a horse stabbed by a foot soldier's yari 'went down like a stone'. Techniques were developed to enable the samurai to use this weapon in any situation: from a horse, in a charge on foot, or defending castle walls. Some illustrations suggest that the spears were used from the saddle like lances, others that they were more often used for making slashing strokes while standing up in the stirrups.

After the initial exchange of gunfire and arrows, the Kawanakajima battlefields would largely be a scene of spear fighting by both samurai and ashigaru, although some adepts would be seen whirling their naginata. If a samurai was observed using a sword then it was likely that his spear shaft had broken or that he was an expert swordsman who wished to demonstrate his skills. If two rival samurai began grappling hand-to-hand then it would be probably a *tanto* (dagger), or even bare hands, that decided the outcome.

THE INVASION OF SHINANO

Until the early 1550s the entire province of Shinano physically separated Takeda Shingen and Uesugi Kenshin. Takeda Shingen had played a decisive role in his father's intervention across the Shinano border at Umi no kuchi in 1536. This action was no different from those seen anywhere in Japan during the Sengoku Period as warlords sought to secure their borders or expand their territory. Takeda Shingen followed in his father's footsteps for the first time in 1542.

The road into Shinano from Shingen's home province left Kai at its northwest tip. From here there were two routes through the mountains, roughly corresponding to the course of the railways today. The Saku valley route, as taken by Takeda Nobutora when he attacked Umi no kuchi in 1536, ran almost due north. Beyond Saku were the headwaters of the Chikumagawa. The alternative route into Shinano took a more northwesterly direction, arriving first at Lake Suwa. From here the mountains could be crossed due north using the Daimon Pass, or bypassed in a long detour around Lake Suwa to join the headwaters of the Saigawa north of present-day Matsumoto.

The Suwa campaign of 1542

In March 1542 Takeda Shingen invaded Shinano along the Suwa route. As a result of previous marriage-based alliances, this was the territory of his brother-in-law, but this did not deter him. His intended victim, Suwa Yorishige, was married to Shingen's sister and ruled lands around Lake Suwa. The territory was protected against attack from Kai province by the two yamashiro of Kuwabara and Uehara. Near Lake Suwa also lay two very important Shinto shrines dedicated to the *kami* Take-minakata-no-mikoto. Suwa Yorishige was the chief priest of the shrines in addition to being a daimyo, but there were political differences between him and the priest of the lower Suwa shrine. A fortuitous disagreement provided the opportunity for Takeda Shingen to intervene.

The other daimyo of Shinano reacted angrily to the Takeda threat against one of their number. When Shingen advanced, Suwa Yorishige, Ogasawara Nagatoki and Murakami Yoshikiyo (all of whom had invaded Kai the previous year) joined forces with Kiso Yoshiyasu from down the Ina valley and tried to stop the Takeda at Sezawa, halfway up the valley to Lake Suwa. However, on 25 March 1542 the Shinano allies were totally defeated:

> *Harunobu's generals had become afraid. Harunobu said, 'There are four of them working together, but they may not necessarily agree among themselves. We should engage them in battle and defeat them'. To fool them Harunobu widened his moat and increased the height of his earthwork walls. The four men regarded this as an expression of cowardice and without hesitation*

Uesugi Kenshin in martial mood, clutching a staff made from green bamboo. This is a detail from a woodblock print depicting Kenshin with his Twenty-Eight Generals.

1. 1536: The Takeda capture Unmi no kuchi.
2. 1542; Takeda Shingen launches his first invasion of Shinano and has to fight an alliance of Shinano daimyo at the battle of Sezawa.
3. Later in 1542 Takeda Shingen returns to Shinano and defeats Suwa Yorishige. Takato Yoritsugu flees.
4. Pursuing Takato Yoritsugu, the Takeda army makes gains in the Ina valley.
5. In 1543 Oi Sadataka deserts the Takeda, prompting Shingen's first expedition along the Saku valley.
6. 1545: Takato Yoritsugu is finally defeated.
7. In June 1546 a major offensive along the Saku valley leads to the sieges of Uchiyama and Shiga. The Ogigayatsu Uésugi intervene but are defeated at the battle of Odaihara (19 September).
8. Further progress north by Shingen in 1548 leads to his defeat by Murakami Yoshikiyo at the battle of Uedahara.
9. Ogasawara Nagatoki tries to capitalise on Shingen's recent defeat at Uedahara, but is himself defeated at the battle of Shiojiritoge (August 1548).
10. August 1550: Takeda Shingen captures the remaining Ogasawara castles.
11. The Murakami stronghold of Toishi falls to an attack by Shingen's general Sanada Yukitaka in 1551.
12. 21 May 1553: Murakami Yoshikiyo's base of Katsurao is taken by the Takeda. Murakami flees to Echigo and the protection of Uesugi Kenshin.
13. 3 June: The first skirmish between Shingen and Kenshin takes place at Hachiman as a response to Murakami Yoshikiyo's call for help.
14. October 1553: The first battle of Kawanakajima is fought at Fuse.
15. September 1553: The Takeda carry out deep probing raids to the west of Kawanakajima along the Itoigawa. At the same time Murakami Yoshikiyo's remaining fortresses of Wada (8 Sept.), Takashima (10 Sept.) and Shioda (12 Sept.) are captured.
16. Following the indecisive second battle of Kawanakajima in 1555, Shingen takes Katsurayama castle in 1557, thus opening up the highlands of Togakushi.
17. A futher raid down the Itoigawa captures Otari for the Takeda. Shortly afterwards Iiyama is besieged. The siege is soon abandoned but it prompts Uesugi Kenshin to launch the raids that lead to the third battle of Kawanakajima.
18. In the years immediately before the fourth battle of Kawanakajima in 1561, Shingen strengthens his position on the east bank of the Chikumagawa by capturing Takanashi and building castles at Amakazari and Kaizu (Matsushiro).
19. Using the high mountain routes, Shingen captures Warigadake castle in 1564.
20. Following the fifth battle of Kawanakajima, Shingen pursues Kenshin only as far as Motodoriyama castle.
21. In 1568 Takeda Shingen strengthens his position at Nagahama on the border between Shinano and Echigo.

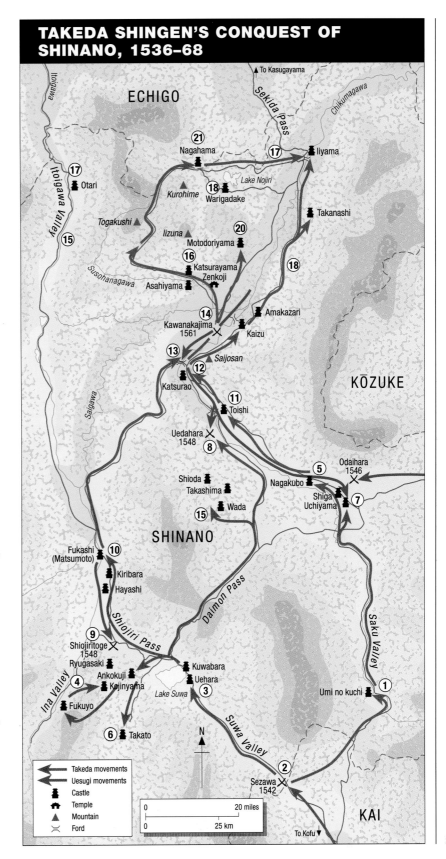

TAKEDA SHINGEN'S CONQUEST OF SHINANO, 1536–68

advanced towards Harunobu's territory. Harunobu marched out during the night and took advantage of the misty rain. He pressed forward and struck, handing the enemy a resounding defeat.

Having made such a fine demonstration of Takeda power, Shingen calmly withdrew to regroup.

He returned to Shinano three months later and marched directly against Suwa Yorishige's positions, and this time no allies appeared to intervene. On 13 August Shingen captured Uehara castle and laid siege to Kuwabara castle the day afterwards. Suwa Yorishige was now in a desperate plight. Not only was he was faced with Shingen's siege but Takato Yoritsugu, his neighbour across the valley, had joined the Takeda against him. Yoritsugu hoped that giving support to Shingen would allow him to become chief priest of the Suwa shrines, a position he had long coveted.

Realising that his situation was hopeless, Suwa Yorishige negotiated with Shingen and surrendered Kuwabara in return for safe conduct. Takeda Shingen sent him to Kofu. His journey thither was safe enough, but once he was securely inside Tsutsujigasaki Takeda Shingen ordered Yorishige, his own brother-in-law, to commit hara kiri.

As a reward for his betrayal of his neighbour, Takato Yoritsugu received half the Suwa lands. He did not receive the position of chief priest of the Suwa shrine, however. Enraged at this, Yoritsugu invaded the other half of the territory that was now in Takeda hands. Shingen cleverly made Suwa Yorishige's son the nominal leader of the forces of resistance, ensuring Takato Yoritsugu received no support from the former Suwa retainers. Instead, in October 1542 Takeda Shingen's general Itagaki Nobukata captured Yoritsugu's castle of Ankokuji and killed his brother Yorimune. Takato Yoritsugu fled south along the Ina valley to take refuge with Fujizawa Yorichika in Fukuyo castle. Shingen's vanguard under Komai Masatake then crossed the Tsuetsuki Pass and captured Fukuyo. Yoritsugu escaped again and ensconced himself in Kojinyama. This was much a safer refuge, and it was to be 1544 before

the Takeda caught up with him again.

He was, however, far enough away not to threaten Shingen's occupation of the Suwa area, which was a valuable prize for the Takeda. It was to provide a useful jumping-off point for several of Shingen's future Shinano adventures. Shingen also took the late Yorishige's daughter as his mistress. Taking one's own niece, whose father you have had murdered, as a mistress was not an auspicious move. Tongues wagged, and people said that no good would come of it. The lady of Suwa was indeed destined to bring nemesis to the house of Takeda – she bore Shingen a son called Katsuyori, who would lead his clan to destruction in 1575 at the famous battle of Nagashino.

The Saku and Ina campaigns, 1543–47

Further gains were made when Takeda Shingen's local ally Oi Sadataka, the keeper of Nagakubo castle in the Saku area, deserted the Takeda cause in 1543. Such disloyalty could not be forgiven, so Shingen entered Saku via the Suwa route, crossing the mountains to drop down on Nagakubo. The castle fell and Oi Sadataka was sent as a prisoner to Kofu, where he was killed.

Shingen's progress northward into Shinano was then temporarily interrupted while he put paid to Takato Yoritsugu, who was still skulking in the Ina valley. Kojinyama castle fell in October 1544, and in May 1545 Takeda Shingen captured Yoritsugu's own castle of Takato. Ryugasaki, a satellite yamashiro across the valley from Kojinyama, fell to Takeda Shingen in July 1545, thus placing the whole area immediately to the south of Lake Suwa firmly in Takeda hands.

The Saku campaign resumed in June 1546 when Shingen marched against Uchiyama castle, held by Oi Sadakiyo, son of the late Sadataka. He captured it by starving out the garrison. The following year's target was Shiga (sometimes written as Shika), commanded by Kasahara Kiyoshige, which proved to be a tougher proposition. The siege began on 8 September 1547, but the castle held out stubbornly even when

In this snapshot of the Takeda departure for war festival in Kofu we see a re-enactment of the Sanada contingent, who look remarkably cheerful as they march off to fight for the Takeda.

Shingen cut off its water supply and condemned the garrison to a slow and dreadful death from thirst.

Kasahara Kiyoshige's optimism was based on information that Uesugi Norimasa would soon march in from Kozuke province and relieve him. His confidence was well founded, and Uesugi forces totalling 3,000 men led by Kanai Hidekage soon crossed the Usui Pass from Kozuke. Leaving part of his army to continue the siege of Shiga, Takeda Shingen sent Itagaki Nobukata and others to meet the relieving army. They destroyed the Kozuke force on 19 September at the battle of Odaihara, but still the defiant Kasahara would not surrender. Shingen's next action is a chilling example of psychological warfare. At Odaihara his army had collected the heads from about 15 senior samurai and 300 ashigaru and these grisly trophies were now mounted on spear shafts and paraded in front of Shiga castle. Portrayed with great effectiveness in the film *Furin Kazan*, this event confirmed that no relieving army was on its way. At noon on 23 September a fire started within the castle, and that night an assault began during which the brave Kasahara Kiyoshige was killed. Over 200 of the Shiga garrison joined him in death. Their women and children were rounded up and sent to Kofu as slaves.

The battle of Uedahara, 1548

The capture of Shiga brought Takeda-controlled territory into close proximity with the lands of Murakami Yoshikiyo, the strongest daimyo in Shinano and a man whose name will loom large in our story. Yoshikiyo's main castle was called Katsurao. It lay beside the Chikumagawa about two-thirds of the way downstream from Shiga to Kawanakajima. During the second lunar month of 1548 Murakami Yoshikiyo mobilised his forces and led an army south to drive the Takeda out of Shinano. When news reached Kofu, an army under the personal command of Takeda Shingen set out to join the force that had captured Shiga. The stage was set for a momentous battle, and the first defeat of Shingen's career.

The main Takeda army set out on from Kofu on 10 March, advanced along the Suwa route and crossed the Daimon Pass in heavy snow. Yoshikiyo crossed the Chikumagawa and advanced to meet Shingen's army on 23 March at Uedahara ('the moor of Ueda') near present-day Ueda city. Each side numbered about 7,000 men, but the Takeda troops were exhausted from their long march in cold weather from Kofu. Nevertheless, they attacked with their customary gusto in a classic Takeda mounted advance.

Itagaki Nobukata, who led Shingen's vanguard, met the Murakami vanguard head on, but the Murakami absorbed the Takeda charge within their ranks and surrounded them. Itagaki Nobukata died fighting and the Murakami army then counterattacked the Takeda main body. Two prominent Takeda leaders, Amari Torayasu and Hajikano Den'emon were also killed in action. Even Shingen himself was involved in the hand-to-hand spear fighting and was wounded in his left arm. The fight eventually degenerated into a stalemate as the two sides settled down in prepared positions. Although either side was ready to respond to a move by the other, after 20 days fighting had not resumed so Takeda Shingen withdrew to Kofu and Murakami Yoshikiyo let him go. Shingen lost 700 Takeda soldiers killed at Uedahara. *Koyo Gunkan* nonetheless records it as a victory, although other chronicles are more realistic. *Myohoji-ki* records that 'the grief in the province was unending'.

The re-enactment of the Takeda departure for war takes place every year during the annual spring festival at Kofu. Here we see the Takeda samurai resting prior to marching past the figure of Takeda Shingen.

Of interest is Murakami Yoshikiyo's use of Chinese handguns at the battle of Uedahara as a response to the devastating power of the Takeda cavalry. An account appears in *Koyo Gunkan* in the form of a report given by Yoshikiyo to Uesugi Kenshin after the battle:

> *As defence against the horsemen I chose two hundred skilled marksmen out of the army and to one hundred and fifty soldiers I gave five well-made arrows and a bow. And to the remaining fifty ashigaru I gave firearms imported in the seventh year of Eisho with three bullets per man. They were ordered to shoot when they were told and then to discard them and fight with their swords. I ordered the gunners to fire after the arrows had been shot, and placed an officer in charge of every five men.*

The reference to the date (1510) allows us to identify these guns very precisely as simple short-barrelled handguns of Chinese type, originally introduced to Japan in that year. The difference between their use and the Portuguese arquebuses, introduced to Japan only five years before Uedahara, is illustrated by Murakami's orders to his gunners to fire the guns, discard them and use their swords. The days of organised firearm squads had not yet arrived, but Murakami's willingness to experiment shows that he was a leader to be reckoned with.

Ogasawara Nagatoki was another Shinano daimyo to be reckoned with. He was based northwest of Lake Suwa at Fukashi castle in present-day Matsumoto city. Nagatoki had supported the unfortunate Takato Yoritsugu when Takeda Shingen invaded the Ina valley in 1544. At the time he had failed to prevent the loss of the Suwa area, but, heartened by the news of Uedahara, Ogasawara Nagatoki lent his support to fresh moves to drive out the Takeda. He first joined forces with the Murakami to follow up the triumph at Uedahara by attacking Takeda outposts near Lake Suwa. On 1 June the allied Shinano forces burned down the main Takeda base in the Saku valley at Uchiyama, but Shingen's general Oyamada Nobushige regained it in September.

Ogasawara Nagatoki's next move against the Takeda was even less successful. He marched southeast from Fukashi over the Shiojiritoge (Shiojiri Pass) in May 1548 and waited in the pass where he had the advantage of high ground, watching for a response from Shingen. The Takeda army eventually arrived in August and halted for six days without apparently doing anything. On the seventh night Shingen organised a midnight advance: the horses were given straw sandals, and the skirt pieces of the soldiers' suits of armour were tied up with cord so that they would not rattle. Shingen then waited for the dawn before launching his men in a furious assault into the Ogasawara camp. Many Ogasawara samurai had no time to put on their armour and fled in panic back down the pass towards Hayashi castle, the nearest point of safety. The battle of Shiojiritoge was ample revenge for Uedahara.

The road to Kawanakajima

The year 1550 saw a renewed advance by Takeda Shingen into Shinano. Ogasawara Nagatoki was the first to suffer and in August the three Ogasawara fortresses of Hayashi, Kiribara and Fukashi fell in quick succession. Shingen's general Baba Nobuharu was placed in charge of Fukashi, which is now the site of the castle of Matsumoto, one of the most beautiful in Japan. Ogasawara Nagatoki fled for his life and took refuge over the mountains with Murakami Yoshikiyo.

Takeda Shingen's move against the formidable Murakami Yoshikiyo was likely to be a more serious affair, and so it proved. The key to the middle Chikumagawa valley was the Murakami castle of Toishi. If Shingen could capture it Toishi would be a vital base for launching the final attack on the main Murakami castle of Katsurao. Shingen made very thorough preparations that included trying to persuade Murakami's supporters to defect, then set off against Toishi in September 1550. He entered Suwa and crossed the pass to take up a position at Nagakubo castle across the valley from Toishi. On the morning of 4 October scouts were sent out, and Shingen finally advanced to prepared siege lines round Toishi on 9 October when the first arrows were fired into the castle. On the evening of 18 October eight days of intensive fighting began, but Toishi held out against all the Takeda assaults.

On 9 November the Takeda abandoned the siege and began to withdraw to Kofu, at which the Toishi garrison flung open their gates and attacked them in the rear. To add insult to injury Murakami Yoshikiyo, whom the Takeda had believed to be inside the castle inspiring his men, launched a surprise attack from outside, killing Shingen's general Yokota Takatoshi. It was only the quality of Shingen's rearguard that saved them from a total disaster. The army arrived back in Kofu on 15 November. Rai San'yo's account praises Shingen's celebrated general Yamamoto Kansuke Haruyuki for diverting the Murakami attack:

Haruyuki spoke up, 'My lord, do not try to stop the enemy's assault head-on. Make them veer to the right and we will win.' Harunobu answered, 'Even my own soldiers do not always obey my commands, so how can I possibly influence the enemy's own movements?' Haruyuki asked to borrow soldiers from the rear ranks and struck out towards the left. Yoshikiyo's army veered to the right. Harunobu's army's spirits lifted. They pressed forward and repelled the enemy.

Whatever the Takeda chroniclers may have said, Murakami Yoshikiyo had now defeated Takeda Shingen twice. Shingen remained as determined as ever and returned to the Saku valley in 1551. In the fifth lunar month of that year Toishi castle finally fell to an attack by Sanada Yukitaka, one of Shingen's ablest generals. Yukitaka's involvement was in some ways appropriate, because he was a Shinano man forced to flee as a ronin (masterless samurai) into Kozuke when Shingen's 1541 campaign removed his lord. He had submitted to the Takeda as a way of regaining what his family had lost, and his military skills had led to a rapid promotion. Sanada Yukitaka's familiarity with the area may well have contributed to his victory, but it was nevertheless a hard-won fight, although details are sadly lacking. The Murakami casualties reached 1,000 men.

As expected, the control of Toishi made Katsurao castle ultimately untenable, but it took another two years of campaigning and the seizure of all the castles around it before Katsurao fell. During the first lunar month of 1553 Shingen's son Takeda Yoshinobu and his younger brother Takeda 'Tenkyu' Nobushige (once their father's favourite, but now fully reconciled with Shingen) led an army out of Kai to take Katsurao. Many Murakami supporters in the vicinity joined Shingen, and the fall of Katsurao came that much easier seven days later. Legend tells us that Yoshikiyo's wife tried to find a boat to cross the Chikumagawa, but that the boatman did not realise that the refugee was his daimyo's wife. She accordingly pulled out her hairpin and let her hair fall down over her shoulders. He then realised that she was a noble lady and took her to safety.

The final act of the preliminary campaign had now been played. Murakami Yoshikiyo fled north into Echigo province, where he found sanctuary with Uesugi Kenshin. Yoshikiyo reported to him that central and southern Shinano were all but lost. The only castle of any importance still held by the Murakami was Shioda, high up in the mountains, along with a few minor castles in its immediate neighbourhood. They were all under threat of attack, and Takeda Shingen's samurai now occupied their own chain of castles along the valleys. He added that the Takeda were now very near to the border with Kenshin's Echigo province and could soon be expected to march down to occupy the strategic flatlands known as Kawanakajima. The Shinano campaign was over, and the Kawanakajima campaign about to begin.

OPPOSING PLANS

The topography of Kawanakajima

With the flight of Murakami Yoshikiyo into Echigo the strategic interest of both sides turned towards the Kawanakajima area. The traditional notion of the five battles of Kawanakajima inevitably lays great emphasis on what happened on the plain between the Chikuma and Sai rivers. This is only part of the story, however, because each of the five battles was only one stage in a series of complex campaigns involving deep penetrative raids into enemy territory and the capture of castles. The secret to understanding the Kawanakajima campaigns therefore lies in the relationship between the plain and the highlands around it, because Kawanakajima is an island of flat land among towering mountains.

Despite the intrusion of modern motorways and towns the overall topography of the area has changed little since the 16th century. The approach to Kawanakajima from the south consists essentially of one river valley that opens out into Kawanakajima between the modern towns of Yashiro and Shinonoi. Kawanakajima has long been fertile land (it is today a centre of fruit growing and market gardening) and was therefore a rich prize for any samurai warlord. Nowadays the Saigawa marks a natural northern boundary, although 400 years ago the smaller Susohanagawa flowed further north to join the Saigawa just before its confluence with the Chikumagawa. It has since changed its course. After leaving Kawanakajima the Chikumagawa curves round to the northeast to become the Shinano River, the longest river on Japan's main island of Honshu.

The topography on the northern side of Kawanakajima is of equal importance in understanding the five campaigns, because the approaches to Kenshin's capital at Kasugayama, Shingen's ultimate target, were not along the river valley but over high mountain passes. It is easier to look at these routes from the point of view of Uesugi Kenshin coming down into the Kawanakajima plain from Echigo. The most easterly route crossed the ridge by the Sekida Pass and dropped down to the Chikumagawa. A few miles upriver towards Kawanakajima was the castle of Iiyama, which was to be a vital base for the Uesugi on several occasions.

Alternatively Kenshin could cross further west following the line of the modern railway through Arai. This would take him to Lake Nojiri, which lay just inside the Shinano border and was guarded by Warigadake castle. From here he could drop down to the east and the Chikumagawa, or head west between Kurohimeyama (6,700ft) and Iizunayama (6,300ft)

The Susohanagawa, one of Kenshin's three defence lines, viewed here from within the gorge that separates Asahiyama (seen here as near vertical slopes) from Katsurayama.

The mountains of the Togakushi area as seen from Zenkoji. The passes through this area were crucial in the strategy of Kawanakajima.

to the area known as Togakushi. A fourth route that skirted round Kurohimeyama to the north could also be used to reach Togakushi. From Togakushi Kenshin would follow the Susohanagawa to descend to the plain between the hills of Katsurayama and Asahiyama, emerging near the great Buddhist temple of Zenkoji. Much of the narrative that follows will be concerned with battles for control of these passes and the mountains that overlooked them.

Uesugi Kenshin's plans

For both Shingen and Kenshin a change of tremendous proportions took place between 21 May, when Katsurao fell, and the battle of Hachiman on

A re-enactment of Uesugi Kenshin's departure for war takes place annually at Yonezawa. Here we see Kenshin and his generals lined up in front of the *maku* (field curtain) that bears the Uesugi *mon* (badge).

3 June, both in terms of their military positions and their own immediate strategic plans. With the benefit of hindsight we can see that the military situation had changed from the last gasp of a 12-year-long Shinano campaign directed by Shingen against a collection of comparatively minor warlords, to the start of an 11-year-long struggle against one of Japan's most powerful daimyo, with neither Shingen or Kenshin giving ground.

Kenshin's immediate plans focussed on helping Murakami Yoshikiyo, and barely 12 days passed before an Uesugi army was establishing field positions only a few miles away from Katsurao. Kenshin's immediate objective was to crush the advancing Takeda before they threatened Echigo itself. That is the essence of the five battles of Kawanakajima. Takeda Shingen's advance northwards, which had proceeded slowly but inexorably since 1542, was stopped dead in its tracks despite five attempts to break through into Echigo.

In modern terms we would say that Uesugi Kenshin did this by using defence in depth. His castles and field positions represented a continually changing defensive line that he rushed to establish each time Shingen made a move in his direction. He also made extensive use of deep probing raids to entice Shingen into engaging him in a decisive battle. As a result, each of the five encounters was very different. It was not the simplistic scenario of the renowned Takeda cavalry repeatedly beating their heads against strong defence, characteristic of the battle of Nagashino in 1575. The five battles of Kawanakajima represent something far more interesting – a repeated return to a battlefield situation that kept re-inventing itself.

Takeda Shingen's plans

For Takeda Shingen the events of the middle of the fourth lunar month of 1553 represented no change in his overall plans. Instead the 12 days between the fall of Katsurao and the battle of Hachiman were a seamless transition from one target to another in his 12-year-long campaign to conquer Shinano. The intervention of Uesugi Kenshin brought an entirely new factor into the equation, but it can hardly have been unexpected. Shingen must have known that he was drawing near the borders of a rival daimyo every bit as formidable as himself. Nevertheless, it took the experience of what became known as the first battle of Kawanakajima for him to appreciate fully what he was now up against. The plans on which Takeda based the epic Kawanakajima campaign grew therefore from this first-round contest, rather than being developed with such an encounter in mind.

THE STRUGGLE FOR KAWANAKAJIMA

Of all the battles of Kawanakajima, the events of the opening encounter between Shingen and Kenshin are the most difficult to follow. Few written records exist, so there are no precise details about what actually happened during the series of encounters in 1553, one of which, the battle of Fuse on 29 September, is conventionally regarded as 'the first battle of Kawanakajima'. Yet this battle was just one stage in a fluid contest over many miles and several months.

THE FIRST BATTLE OF KAWANAKAJIMA, 1553

The first Kawanakajima campaign began with a rapid advance by Uesugi Kenshin on to the Kawanakajima plain in response to Murakami Yoshikiyo's request for help. Part of the reason for his decision to move so rapidly was surely his desire to catch Takeda Shingen while he was still pursuing Murakami stragglers in the area. When he failed to find him at Kawanakajima, however, Kenshin pressed on into the southern valley towards Katsurao. He located his quarry at a place called Hachiman, so the opening of hostilities between Shingen and Kenshin may be very precisely located in time to 3 June 1553 and in place to Hachiman, a few miles south of Kawanakajima. Hachiman was downstream and across the river from Katsurao, and now lies within the modern town of Yashiro. The name may indicate no more than that there was a shrine to Hachiman the war god at that spot on the western bank of the Chikumagawa.

Following the 1553 encounter Kenshin placed three rivers between himself and Shingen to guard the passes into Echigo. The Chikumagawa was the first line of defence. Then came the Saigawa, but there was also the third river, called the Susohanagawa. This is the confluence of the Saigawa and Susohanagawa, with Nagano seen in the distance.

FIRST BATTLE OF KAWANAKAJIMA, 1553

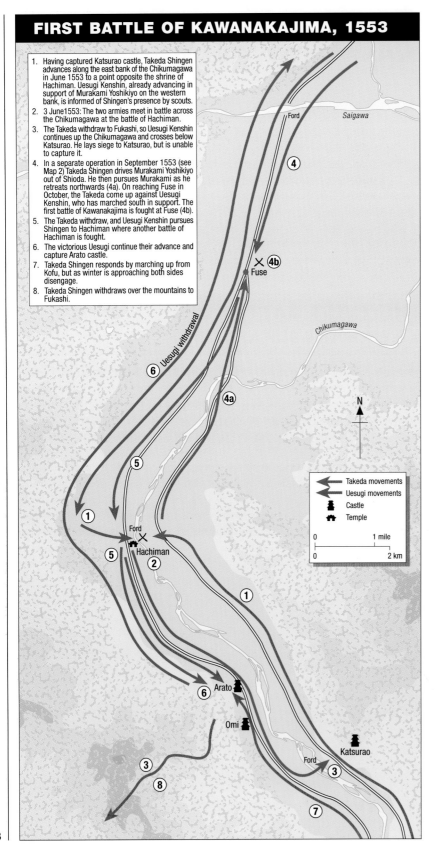

1. Having captured Katsurao castle, Takeda Shingen advances along the east bank of the Chikumagawa in June 1553 to a point opposite the shrine of Hachiman. Uesugi Kenshin, already advancing in support of Murakami Yoshikiyo on the western bank, is informed of Shingen's presence by scouts.

2. 3 June 1553: The two armies meet in battle across the Chikumagawa at the battle of Hachiman.

3. The Takeda withdraw to Fukashi, so Uesugi Kenshin continues up the Chikumagawa and crosses below Katsurao. He lays siege to Katsurao, but is unable to capture it.

4. In a separate operation in September 1553 (see Map 2) Takeda Shingen drives Murakami Yoshikiyo out of Shioda. He then pursues Murakami as he retreats northwards (4a). On reaching Fuse in October, the Takeda come up against Uesugi Kenshin, who has marched south in support. The first battle of Kawanakajima is fought at Fuse (4b).

5. The Takeda withdraw, and Uesugi Kenshin pursues Shingen to Hachiman where another battle of Hachiman is fought.

6. The victorious Uesugi continue their advance and capture Arato castle.

7. Takeda Shingen responds by marching up from Kofu, but as winter is approaching both sides disengage.

8. Takeda Shingen withdraws over the mountains to Fukashi.

Saigawa

Ford

Chikumagawa

Uesugi withdrawal

Fuse

N

Takeda movements
Uesugi movements
Castle
Temple

0   1 mile
0   2 km

Ford
Hachiman

Arato

Omi

Katsurao

Ford

The mountain of Asahiyama as seen from Nagano. In 1555 Takeda Shingen sent reinforcements to strengthen his vital possession of Asahiyama. The 3,000-strong army included 800 archers and 300 men armed with arquebuses. This is the first we read of either Shingen or Kenshin making use of what is apparently a modern firearms squad.

Takeda Shingen had clearly not rested on his laurels after capturing Katsurao, but had begun consolidating his new presence in the former Murakami territories, extending his forward position as far down the eastern bank of the Chikumagawa as he dared. Hachiman was the point of deepest penetration by the Takeda into Shinano up to that time.

Shingen's forward scouts at Hachiman reported that an Uesugi army was on the opposite bank, and a skirmish was fought across the river beside the shrine. The Uesugi army at Hachiman is recorded as being 5,000 men strong, and the victory is credited to Kenshin. Unfortunately, that is all we know about this fateful first encounter. Shingen's vanguard troops may have been the only Takeda representatives at Hachiman, but subsequent events indicate that both Murakami Yoshikiyo and Kenshin were present on the other side.

Having flexed his muscles at Hachiman, Kenshin continued his progress up the west bank of the Chikumagawa, and we may presume that

The opening of hostilities between Shingen and Kenshin may be located to Hachiman, a few miles south of Kawanakajima. Hachiman was downstream and across the river from Katsurao, and now lies within the modern town of Yashiro, between the two bridges shown here.

the Takeda stayed on the opposite eastern bank for the rest of the operation. The next we read is that Kenshin has crossed the river and attacked Katsurao, where he killed the Takeda commander Oso Gempachiro but failed to capture the castle. This was a further act of provocation to add to the victory at Hachiman, but Takeda Shingen did not rise to the bait. He was not yet ready to engage the Uesugi in a full-scale contest. Instead he withdrew in good order to Baba Nobuharu's castle of Fukashi (Matsumoto).

With the Takeda gone from his former territories above the Daimon Pass the bold Murakami Yoshikiyo marched in pursuit to take advantage of the situation. He re-entered Shioda castle and proceeded to drive away any former Murakami supporters who may have declared for the Takeda. The focus then shifted to the area around Shioda.

The siege of Shioda castle, 8–12 September 1553

Takeda Shingen returned to the fray in Shinano three months later, leaving Kofu on 2 September. This time his objectives were different. Instead of advancing down the Chikumagawa he ordered attacks on the remaining Murakami positions around Shioda. On 8 September the Takeda attacked and took Wada, then on 10 September nearby Takashima fell. In both cases the entire garrison was slaughtered as a dreadful warning to the other Murakami garrisons, but there was only one big Murakami castle left. This was Shioda, where Murakami Yoshikiyo had so bravely re-established himself; but discretion was the better part of valour. It would do no good to the future cause of the Murakami if their daimyo was caught defending an isolated castle in a hopeless position. Therefore, when faced with a Takeda advance on 12 September Yoshikiyo fled from Shinano once again. On that same day no less than 16 other Murakami outposts surrendered. The Takeda troops pillaged the area, seizing women and children, and the Takeda general Obu Toramasa was placed in charge of Shioda.

The events of 1553 so far had produced very mixed results, and matters became even more complicated when in early October Takeda

The site of the skirmish at Hachiman from the west. The name may indicate no more than that there was a shrine to Hachiman the war god at this spot on the western bank of the Chikumagawa.

Fuse, located to the north of the present-day town of Shinonoi, lies within the triangle of the Chikumagawa and the Saigawa. The battle of Fuse is therefore regarded as the first battle of Kawanakajima. The mountains in the distance include Saijosan.

Shingen and Uesugi Kenshin fought another battle. This was the battle of Fuse, located a few miles north of Hachiman within the present-day town of Shinonoi, an important modern railway junction. The location is significant, because, unlike the earlier encounter at Hachiman, Fuse lies within the triangle of the Chikumagawa and the Saigawa. Fuse is therefore regarded as the first battle of Kawanakajima.

It is strange to record that we do not even know the actual date of the first battle of Kawanakajima at Fuse, nor can we do more than speculate as to the events that brought Shingen and Kenshin together. Perhaps Takeda Shingen had followed up Murakami Yoshikiyo's withdrawal and encountered Kenshin advancing to provide protection? This is not an unreasonable conclusion, but details of the engagement are sadly lacking. All we know is that Uesugi Kenshin was victorious for a second time that year, stopping Takeda Shingen at his newest point of deepest penetration northwards. More was to come, because 8 October found

Uesugi Kenshin at the second battle of Kawanakajima, sitting confidently on the bank of the Saigawa. Essentially, two huge armies on the battlefield itself engaged in a series of skirmishes and minor operations, but otherwise just glared at each other.

the two commanders back at Hachiman for a second fight. As this must have happened only a few days after Kenshin's victory at Fuse we may assume that Kenshin was pursuing Shingen on his retreat homewards. Kenshin was again victorious – and for the third time that year!

The Takeda fell back once more, so Kenshin pressed on up the west bank of the Chikumagawa and the nearby Takeda possession of Arato castle fell into his hands without a fight. On 10 October the vanguard of the Uesugi army set fire to buildings in the area and captured the minor outpost of Omi, but it was time for Shingen to hit back. On 20 October he attacked and set fire to Arato and Omi. The Uesugi responded four days later by raiding and burning the area around Sakaki, but there were no more battles in that epic year of 1553. Winter was fast approaching, and the Uesugi began their withdrawal sometime around the beginning of November. We may be more precise about Shingen's movements because we know that he was back in Shioda on 12 November. From there he withdrew to Fukashi and arrived safely in Kofu on 22 November.

The momentous sequence of events of 1553 thus came to an end. The 'rolling campaign' had taught each commander some valuable lessons. Both realised that the reputation the other possessed was fully justified, but in terms of immediate response Kenshin's decisions are more revealing. Just before leaving for Kasugayama at the onset of winter, Kenshin ordered the construction of two new castles on the hills of Katsurayama and Motodoriyama immediately to the north of Kawanakajima. Their location is very interesting, because it confirms that Uesugi Kenshin fully appreciated that when Shingen returned to the fray Kawanakajima would be their front line. He had therefore placed three rivers between himself and Shingen to guard the passes into Echigo. The Chikumagawa was the first line of defence. Then came the Saigawa, but there was also the third river called the Susohanagawa. It had a strategic value that is not so apparent these days because its course has changed completely from 1553 and now enters the Saigawa within Nagano city. In 1553 the Susohanagawa was the forward moat for the area of flat land immediately south of the important Buddhist foundation of Zenkoji. With Katsurayama castle overlooking it, and Motodoriyama castle to the rear along the road to Iiyama and Echigo, Kenshin had established defence in depth. He now awaited Shingen's return.

THE SECOND BATTLE OF KAWANAKAJIMA, 1555

The year 1554 was to see no further activity on the Kawanakajima front. Instead Takeda Shingen completed his conquest of the Ina valley by defeating Takato Yoritsugu and Kiso Yoshiyasu. This safeguarded his rear for further advances towards Kawanakajima.

The Itoigawa valley and Zenkoji, spring and summer 1555
The second phase of the struggle between Shingen and Kenshin for control of the 'no-man's land' of Kawanakajima got under way in 1555.

The first fighting began when Shingen ordered a local supporter to attack

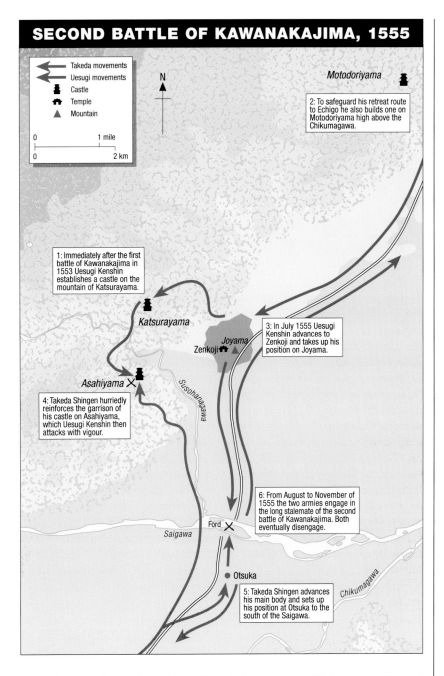

SECOND BATTLE OF KAWANAKAJIMA, 1555

Legend:
- Takeda movements
- Uesugi movements
- Castle
- Temple
- Mountain

0 — 1 mile
0 — 2 km

Motodoriyama

2: To safeguard his retreat route to Echigo he also builds one on Motodoriyama high above the Chikumagawa.

1: Immediately after the first battle of Kawanakajima in 1553 Uesugi Kenshin establishes a castle on the mountain of Katsurayama.

Katsurayama

Joyama
Zenkoji

3: In July 1555 Uesugi Kenshin advances to Zenkoji and takes up his position on Joyama.

Asahiyama ✕

4: Takeda Shingen hurriedly reinforces the garrison of his castle on Asahiyama, which Uesugi Kenshin then attacks with vigour.

Susohanagawa

6: From August to November of 1555 the two armies engage in the long stalemate of the second battle of Kawanakajima. Both eventually disengage.

Ford ✕

Saigawa

• Otsuka

Chikumagawa

5: Takeda Shingen advances his main body and sets up his position at Otsuka to the south of the Saigawa.

Uesugi possessions along the valley of the Itoigawa. This caused Uesugi Kenshin great concern, even though this route lay a long way over the mountains to the west, because the Itoigawa flowed due north to enter the Sea of Japan to the west of Kasugayama. It was therefore the backdoor route to Kenshin's capital, and the raids were a warning that if Shingen was not stopped Kenshin might one day find him at the gates of Kasugayama.

Kenshin's response came in July 1555 when he led an army across the Shinano border and set up camp in a position that reflected the defence in depth that he had created north of the Susohana River. The chronicles name his base as Zenkoji, but a more likely candidate is a hill called

The temple of Zenkoji is one of the holiest Buddhist sanctuaries in Japan. Its main hall houses a statue called the Amida triad. Zenkoji was apparently Kenshin's headquarters during the second battle of Kawanakajima, although the hill of Joyama slightly to the east is more likely to have been its exact location.

Joyama a little to the east. It is unlikely that Kenshin would choose to risk the fate of the great Buddhist foundation of Zenkoji by establishing an army camp in its grounds.

The temple of Zenkoji, which was shortly to witness much fierce fighting, is one of the holiest Buddhist sanctuaries in Japan. Its main hall houses a statue called the Amida triad, which consists of three figures of Amida Buddha sharing one halo. The image is never seen. Instead an exact replica is put on show once every seven years in an impressive festival. Part of its significance is that the image is believed to be the first Buddhist statue ever to arrive in Japan. This important event happened in 552, and the statue's earliest fate was to be unceremoniously dumped in a canal. It was rescued by Honda Yoshimitsu and installed at his hometown in Shinano. Zenko is the Chinese reading of Yoshimitsu.

In 1555 Zenkoji stood on a hill from which there was a distant view of the Susohana and Sai rivers that protected it from the triangle of Kawanakajima. Across the valley lay more hills, the Chikumagawa and the pass through which Takeda Shingen would emerge from Kai.

The site of the second battle of Kawanakajima looking east along the Saigawa from the modern road bridge. More than any other event in the 11-year saga of their confrontations at Kawanakajima, this second battle across the Saigawa in 1555 has given rise to the popular image of Kawanakajima as a series of mock battles.

Unfortunately for Kenshin the head of the Zenkoji priesthood was traditionally one of the Kurita family, who were sympathetic to Shingen, and when the Uesugi army arrived on Joyama, Kurita Kakuju slipped away secretly from Zenkoji to his nearby castle on Asahiyama. It was not far away, but its importance lay in the fact that it was across the Susohanagawa from Zenkoji, and thus acted as a Takeda outpost right on Kenshin's front line.

Takeda Shingen, who was already on his way to Kawanakajima, immediately sent reinforcements to strengthen his vital possession of Asahiyama. The 3,000-strong army included 800 archers and 300 men armed with arquebuses. This is the first we read of either Shingen or Kenshin making use of what is apparently a modern firearms squad, and represents an important development in samurai warfare.

Stalemate at the Saigawa, 4 August–27 November 1555

The Takeda main body advanced across the Chikumagawa and took up position across the Saigawa from Zenkoji at a place called Otsuka. Uesugi Kenshin marched down to oppose him, and 4 August 1555 was to find the Takeda and Uesugi fighting each other across the Saigawa on the first day of an encounter that is known to history as the Second Battle of Kawanakajima.

There was no immediate result from the first two days of fighting, and the battle subsided into a stalemate and cautious manoeuvring that

A stylised version of one of the battles of Kawanakajima is shown here in an elaborate print. The right-hand side is missing, but the remaining panels show how a contemporary army could have been drawn up.

was to last for nearly four months. Throughout this time the letters of commendation and other correspondence issued by both commanders from the field positions they had erected make it clear that most of the fighting happened at places other than the banks of the Saigawa. Uesugi Kenshin launched one particularly furious assault across the Susohanagawa against Asahiyama, but Shingen's arquebuses proved their worth and no impression was made on the fortress. By way of contrast, two huge armies on the battlefield itself engaged in a series of skirmishes and minor operations, but otherwise just glared menacingly at each other.

More than any other event in the 11-year saga of their confrontations at Kawanakajima, this second battle in 1555 has given rise to the popular

Takeda Shingen at the second battle of Kawanakajima. His messenger is kneeling in front of him. The Saigawa appears behind them. There may not have been a decisive battle, but the four months of fighting before the armies disengaged were real enough.

Another print shows Takeda Shingen in command at the second battle of Kawanakajima. In the end it was the demands of agriculture rather than the battlefield that prevailed upon both sides to withdraw from the stalemate at the Saigawa.

Uesugi Kenshin from a painted scroll in the Koyasan Treasure House. He is wearing a suit of armour with a cock's feather *sashimono* and a helmet with a white horsehair fringe.

image of Kawanakajima as a series of mock battles. There was some fighting in midstream as the vanguard of one army tried to entice the other to engage them, but each commander was waiting for the other to make a mistake from which some genuine advantage could be gained. The situation at the second battle of Kawanakajima was that of two evenly matched armies facing each other across a wide riverbed that gave them few advantages and even fewer opportunities. In contrast to the war of movement that had characterised the furious series of events in 1553, 1555 was a static war when both sides were trapped by their own skill.

It is nonetheless most unlikely that the ordinary samurai encamped beside the Saigawa believed they were taking part in a mock battle. A better analogy is perhaps the situation in the trenches of World War I. One particular parallel was Uesugi Kenshin's policy of launching raids every night to prevent boredom. On one occasion Takeda Shingen responded by mobilising over 1,000 men for a night attack on the Zenkoji position. This turned out to be a failure. Another raid consisted of an Uesugi attack on Shingen's supply train bringing rice from Kai. There may not have been a decisive battle, but the four months of fighting were real enough.

In the end it was the demands of agriculture rather than the battlefield that prevailed upon both sides to withdraw. These were the days when many samurai were part-time farmers too, and the ashigaru were urgently needed in the fields. Peace was settled on 27 November and the last contingents of both armies finally withdrew. As part of the conditions of separation the castle of Asahiyama was demolished, so the second battle of Kawanakajima came to an end.

THE THIRD BATTLE OF KAWANAKAJIMA, 1557

The third battle of Kawanakajima came about in 1557 when Takeda Shingen's army carried out its furthest penetration into Uesugi territory. It is one of the least well known of all the Kawanakajima battles, but is also one of the most interesting, even though the stalemate with which it concluded is monotonously typical.

The siege of Katsurayama, March 1557
Shingen's 1557 strategy was a bold one. His overall aim of the subjugation of Shinano remained, but the new operation involved taking the fight much further beyond Kawanakajima than in 1555. In this Shingen demonstrated that he had learned some lessons from the previous encounter, because in that year he had depended upon the now ruined Asahiyama to provide a front-line yamashiro. Kenshin had built his own Katsurayama castle in 1553 across the Susohanagawa from Asahiyama to guard the entrance to the passes, so in 1557 Katsurayama itself became Shingen's primary target. Its capture would throw the nearby mountainous areas of Iizuna and Togakushi into Shingen's lap and open a high-level route into Echigo.

In March 1557, taking advantage of late snow that kept Uesugi Kenshin temporarily confined behind the passes from Echigo, Takeda Shingen's

The site of Katsurayama castle, one of the most bitterly contested yamashiro in the whole of the Kawanakajima campaign. Katsurayama is the peak to the left. It is divided from Asahiyama by the Susohana River.

general Baba Nobuharu attacked Katsurayama with 6,000 men in a furious battle that was as much a race against time as anything else. The mountains around were themselves covered in snow (the Iizuna area was one of the main skiing centres during the 1998 Winter Olympics), and provided a suitably quiet backdrop to an operation that was savage even by the standards set so far in the Kawanakajima campaign. The garrison of Katsurayama, who were under the command of Ochiai Bitchu no kami, defended the castle desperately, hoping to hold out until the thaw came, and the majority of the defenders eventually died in action. In the numerous *kanjo* (letters of commendation) that Shingen sent out after the battle he refers to the large number of heads taken at Katsurayama. For example, a samurai from Suwa called Chino Yugeinojo had fought for Shingen at each of his Kawanakajima battles and achieved a total to date of eight enemy heads, of which four were taken at the siege of Katsurayama.

A popular anecdote concerning the fall of Katsurayama tells how the castle's greatest weakness was its lack of a water supply. There was no spring on top of the mountain, so all drinking water had to be carried up from a source near the Joshoji temple on the mountain's lower slopes. This fact was initially unknown to the Takeda troops, and as water was always a crucial factor in a siege the garrison decided to fool the besiegers into thinking that they had ample supplies. As they had plenty of rice the Ochiai soldiers chose a place that was easily visible from the Takeda lines and poured out the white rice in a torrent that looked like a waterfall. It boldly proclaimed the message that this desperately defended castle would be able to hold out until Kenshin broke through.

Unfortunately for the Ochiai, the chief priest of Joshoji betrayed their clever scheme. He passed on to the Takeda the secret information that their only source of water in fact lay down beside the temple. Baba Nobuharu's men rushed to occupy the spring and then attacked the castle with renewed confidence. This time they managed to set fire to the castle buildings and the brave castle commander was killed in the attack that followed. There followed a mass suicide by the wives, women and children of the castle, who flung themselves to their deaths from the

This is a reproduction, flying proudly on the site of the fourth battle of Kawanakajima, of Takeda Shingen's famous banner containing a quotation from Son Zi, the adopted motto of the Takeda.

crags. The castle burned to ashes, so that 'even now when the site is dug, baked rice may be found'.

This vivid legend cannot however be linked unequivocally to Katsurayama. There are similar stories told about other sieges, one of which, concerning the siege of Toksan in Korea in 1593 has the defending general washing his horse with white rice. As for finding baked rice on the Katsurayama site, this would be by no means an unusual discovery where a yamashiro had been burned to ashes and taken its rice store with it. Nevertheless, it is clear that Katsurayama fell only after a long and desperate struggle.

Shingen on the Echigo border, spring 1557

The Takeda followed up the victory by advancing deeper into the mountains and seizing the fortress of Nagahama, held for the Uesugi by the Shimazu family. Other local Uesugi supporters fled to Echigo. This was a very important gain for the Takeda, because Nagahama lay almost on the Echigo border and controlled another of the passes down into Uesugi territory. The seizure of this area also yielded an unusual prize for the Takeda, because deep in these mountains in a place called Togakushi lies a shrine dedicated to the Sun Goddess Amaterasu o mikami. The shrine is associated with one of the best-known stories in the Shinto creation myths, as it is believed to mark the position of the cave into which Amaterasu withdrew and

Baba Nobuharu, who captured Katsurayama after a fierce winter siege, appears at top right in this scroll of the Takeda Twenty-Four Generals. He is shown with Naito Masatoyo (lower right).

from which she was enticed by the local population to bring back sunshine to the world. The new Takeda territory was more than a jumping-off point for a future invasion of Echigo – it was holy ground.

In the early spring of 1557 more earthly considerations were filling the minds of the two protagonists. Kenshin's defence line, which he had carefully anchored on a series of rivers and castles, had now been completely outflanked. Motodoriyama castle behind Zenkoji still remained in Uesugi hands, as did Iiyama, but the Takeda could now bypass the Chikumagawa valley route completely. The route from Togakushi would allow them to cross the mountains via Lake Nojiri and drop down on to Iiyama castle from behind. Takeda Shingen's rapid and cunning winter advance therefore called for a major response from Uesugi Kenshin. We are fortunate that one version of the call to arms issued by Uesugi Kenshin as a response to these incidents is still preserved in the Uesugi family archives. It consists of a letter written by Uesugi Kenshin to Irobe Katsunaga:

Concerning the disturbances among the various families of Shinano and the Takeda of Kai in the year before last, it is the opinion of Imagawa Yoshimoto of Sumpu that things must have calmed down. However, since that time, Takeda Harunobu's example of government has been corrupt and bad. Nevertheless, thanks to the will of the kami and the good offices of Yoshimoto, I, Kagetora, have very patiently avoided any interference. Now, Harunobu has set out for war, and it is a fact that he has torn to pieces the retainers of the Ochiai family of Shinano and Katsurayama

THE SIEGE OF KATSURAYAMA, 1557 (pages 50–51)

The bitter siege of Katsurayama in early 1557 was the opening act of what would culminate in the anti-climactic third battle of Kawanakajima. Here Takeda Shingen's general Baba Nobuharu (1) arrives in the Takeda lines on a neighbouring peak overlooking the Susohanagawa River. Nobuharu was directing operations against Katsurayama castle from down in the valley, and has been urgently summoned to the scene by his forward troops. Across the valley, visible through the steadily falling snow, lies the rough wooden fortress of Katsurayama (2). It is a typical yamashiro castle, built on a cleared mountain peak using wood for its construction and very little stone. The walls are of planking, but there is a strong looking gatehouse (3) and openwork observation towers (4) inside the walls. The Ochiai family garrison the castle under the command of Ochiai Bitchu no kami and on behalf of Uesugi Kenshin, and it is the latter's flags (5) of a red sun's disc on dark blue that fly from the walls. The Takeda samurai are astounded that the Ochiai defenders apparently have such abundant supplies of water that they can afford to pour it away (6) simply to impress their attackers. This was in fact a ruse on the part of the Ochiai garrison. The 'water' was actually rice, and when the truth became known Katsurayama fell after one of the bloodiest battles in samurai history. For now no one can be quite sure what is going on. Baba Nobuharu has been brought to the viewing point in a palanquin (7). This was a simple carrying device like a sedan chair, and only the

highest-ranking generals would use one. He has therefore not dressed against the snow, but wears a splendid suit of armour of a style known as a *mogami-do*. His dagger scabbard (8) is inlaid with mother of pearl. One of his attendant ashigaru protects him from the snow using a large red umbrella (9). Another proudly displays his personal banner (10), which is supported in a leather bucket tied at the man's waist. The flag has an abstract design supposed to represent a mountain path. Baba Nobuharu's used only the flag as his battlefield standard, but examples of umbrellas as standards are known. The ashigaru (11) who have carried Baba Nobuharu up the mountain lack cold weather clothing. They wear simpler two-piece *okegawa-do* suits of armour bearing the Takeda *mon* (badge), and they look exhausted. Their sashimono (back flags) are blue with the Takeda *mon* in black (12). The ashigaru manning the siege lines are better protected against the weather using the traditional winter clothing of the Japanese farmer including head cloths that tie round the face (13). Their feet are kept warm by snow shoes made from bundles of straw (14) that enclosed the shin guards and straw sandals. They also wear the classic shaggy straw raincoats (15) but they are nonetheless very cold. The snow has piled up against their wooden shields (16). These are the usual model constructed of wooden planking with a hinged prop and could stop an arrow. They acted like the pavises of medieval Europe and, although not visible from this angle, the Takeda *mon* would appear on the front. (Wayne Reynolds)

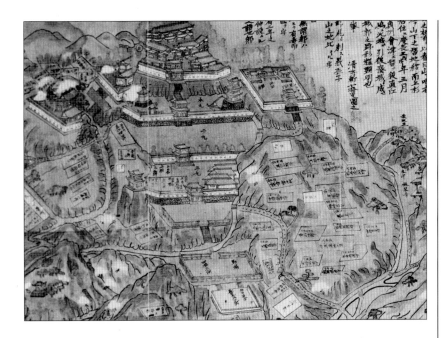

Kasugayama castle, Uesugi Kenshin's headquarters and the ultimate object of every one of Takeda Shingen's campaigns against him. This print shows it as a typical *yamashiro* castle of the period.

castle has fallen. He has moved into the Shimazu and Ogura territories for the time being. My army will turn to face him, and I, Kagetora, will set out for war and meet them half way. In spite of snowstorms or any kind of difficulty we will set out for war, by day or night. I have been waiting for this. If our family's allies in Shinano can be destroyed then even our defences in Echigo will not be safe. Now that things have come to such a pass, assemble your pre-eminent army and be diligent in loyalty. There is honourable work to be done at this time.

With respects
Kenshin
Koji 3, 2m 16d [16 March 1557]

Just as he said in the letter, Uesugi Kenshin set out to meet Shingen half way, and the end result was the third battle of Kawanakajima.

The siege of Iiyama, April 1557

Long before the battle took place, however, a further serious challenge developed, because Takeda Shingen had not stopped at Nagahama but had made good use of his newly acquired control of the Togakushi/Iizuna area to outflank the now isolated Motodoriyama castle and launch an attack on Iiyama castle. The Takeda vanguard was now poised to destroy the most important Uesugi border post.

The message that Takanashi Masayori, the commander of Iiyama, sent to Uesugi Kenshin was couched in appropriately earnest tones. Relief was needed immediately or Iiyama would fall. The closeness of the familial relationship between Kenshin and the Takanashi (they were of his grandmother's family) helped his pleas, so the Uesugi vanguard under Kenshin's brother-in-law Nagao Masakage left Kasugayama around 9 April and later that same month arrived before Iiyama. The Takeda vanguard informed Kofu of the approach of the Uesugi on 10 April and Takeda Shingen set out with his main army. We are not told whether or not the siege of Iiyama

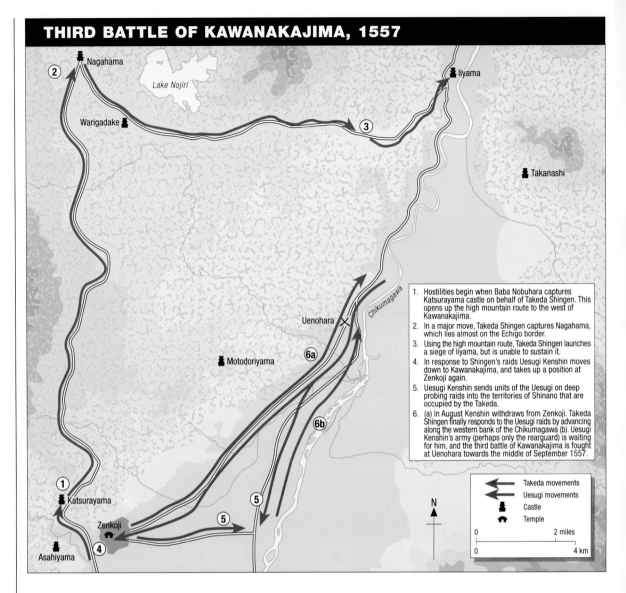

1. Hostilities begin when Baba Nobuhara captures Katsurayama castle on behalf of Takeda Shingen. This opens up the high mountain route to the west of Kawanakajima.
2. In a major move, Takeda Shingen captures Nagahama, which lies almost on the Echigo border.
3. Using the high mountain route, Takeda Shingen launches a siege of Iiyama, but is unable to sustain it.
4. In response to Shingen's raids Uesugi Kenshin moves down to Kawanakajima, and takes up a position at Zenkoji again.
5. Uesugi Kenshin sends units of the Uesugi on deep probing raids into the territories of Shinano that are occupied by the Takeda.
6. (a) In August Kenshin withdraws from Zenkoji. Takeda Shingen finally responds to the Uesugi raids by advancing along the western bank of the Chikumagawa (b). Uesugi Kenshin's army (perhaps only the rearguard) is waiting for him, and the third battle of Kawanakajima is fought at Uenohara towards the middle of September 1557.

	Takeda movements
	Uesugi movements
	Castle
	Temple

was abandoned at this stage, but in view of subsequent developments it is safe to conclude that it was.

The 16th day of May 1557 found Uesugi Kenshin's main body crossing the pass on the border between Echigo and Shinano. On 19 May he arrived at his previous safe haven of Zenkoji, where he attacked nearby Takeda outposts and ordered the restoration of Asahiyama, which he then filled with troops. With Katsurayama menacing them to the northwest Asahiyama was a useful base to hold. Control of these two key castles was now exactly the reverse of the situation in 1555.

From a letter sent by Kenshin from Zenkoji it is clear that his chief desire was a decisive battle with Takeda Shingen. He had experienced two false starts, but from the Uesugi point of view the conditions were now very auspicious. The important decision that Uesugi Kenshin had to make was where to engage Shingen in this decisive battle. The presence of the Takeda at Katsurayama and Togakushi made the Kawanakajima plain below Zenkoji far more vulnerable than it had been in 1555, so Kenshin

A *haramaki* armour (opening at the back) as would have been seen at Kawanakajima. This example has a large *nodowa* (throat guard) and heavy *o-sode* (shoulder guards)

A *do maru* armour (opening at the side) with large *o-sode*. Both this and the above style of armour would have been seen in large numbers at Kawanakajima.

left some troops at Zenkoji and Asahiyama and prudently withdrew a few miles back to Iiyama to wait for Shingen's advance. This, he hoped, would lure Shingen on so that Kenshin could fight him on ground of his own choosing. This ground would be the flat land known as Uenohara beside the Chikumagawa, where Motodoriyama castle would prevent any direct flank attack by Shingen's 'mountain army' and Iiyama castle provided a convenient refuge to the rear. All that Kenshin now had to do was to persuade Shingen to come and fight him at Uenohara.

Shingen's plans are by no means clear, but we do know that he came over the Usui Pass from the direction of Kozuke where he had been campaigning. He set out for Kawanakajima early in June, but he did not completely swallow Kenshin's bait. Instead he kept his main body back near the site of his previous triumph at Odaihara. As for Kenshin, he is recorded as offering up a prayer for victory at a Buddhist temple near Iiyama on the tenth day of the fifth lunar month. Realising that Takeda Shingen was not going to oblige him with an immediate advance, Kenshin moved back down to the Kawanakajima area, but there was still no apparent movement on the part of his rival. It was all very frustrating!

Realising that something far bolder was needed, Uesugi Kenshin sent mounted units of Uesugi troops on a series of raids into Takeda territory. One such raid headed out to the west and took Kosaka castle (modern Shinshu Shinmachi). Another extraordinary raid set off up the Chikumagawa valley, and in a repeat of the 1553 operation the army passed Fuse, Hachiman and Katsurao and attacked the Sakaki area, defeating detachments of Takeda troops and devastating their lands.

The Uesugi raiders finally reached Iwahana, to the northwest of modern Ueda City on 9 June. Here they stopped because there was still no sign of a main body that they could lure back to Kawanakajima. Shingen was very near, but if the raiders advanced any further in that direction they might themselves be caught in the Saku valley. Kenshin informed Takanashi Masayori:

When I began this operation the enemy pulled back three or five ri [9–15 miles] and I made them flee, and it is to my regret that I was not able to destroy them.

Kenshin sadly pulled his men back from the Iwahana area, but soon the encouraging news arrived that Takeda Shingen had begun to follow him very cautiously. This was a pleasing response.

Shingen sent his vanguard on ahead under the command of Yamagata Masakage, one of his finest generals. His mission was however not to attack the Uesugi army but to raid towards Uesugi territory in retaliation for the recent Uesugi operations. Yamagata's endeavours were as bold as his Uesugi counterpart's efforts had been, because we read of him capturing Otari castle, which lay on the Itoi River. This was a remarkable feat, because the Itoigawa flows due north on the other side of the Togakushi area from Kawanakajima to enter the Sea of Japan. We must assume that Yamagata Masakage had headed downstream from Matsumoto, because the alternative approach via Katsurayama and Togakushi would have involved crossing one of the highest ridges of the 'Japan Alps'. The capture of Otari was an operation that seriously alarmed Kenshin, because just as in 1555 Takeda horsemen were poised

to gallop down the Itoigawa to the sea. They were only 25 miles from Kasugayama castle, and were knocking on its back door.

The battle of Uenohara, August–September 1557

Realising that the initiative had passed back to Shingen, the false retreat back to Iiyama that Kenshin had planned to make in order to draw Shingen on now became a genuine withdrawal. At this Takeda Shingen sent his samurai in pursuit. Uesugi Kenshin's original plans thus finally came to fruition and the result was the battle of Uenohara, otherwise known as the third battle of Kawanakajima.

The third battle was fought in the eighth lunar month (between mid-August and mid-September) below Uesugi Kenshin's castle on Motodoriyama near the Chikumagawa, further north than any of the other Kawanakajima battles. It is more than likely that neither army's main body was actually involved at this third battle of Kawanakajima. Instead Uenohara was probably fought only between Shingen's vanguard under Yamagata Masakage and Kenshin's rearguard under Ichikawa Fujiyoshi, a Shinano samurai who had abandoned Shingen for Kenshin a year before. Uesugi Kenshin was probably back in Kasugayama.

Needless to say, that is not how the third battle of Kawanakajima is popularly presented. It is regarded simply as another contest between Shingen and Kenshin, but the historical records cast considerable doubt on this interpretation as it is Uesugi Kenshin's brother-in-law's name that appears on two of the *kanjo* that followed the battle. They are addressed to Ohashi Yajiro and Shimodaira Yashichiro. The one to Shimodaira Yashichiro reads as follows:

In Uenohara in Shinshu, we confronted Harunobu and gave battle; gaining a victory was an unparalleled work of divine mystery. Hereafter may you strive more and more in this important work. Sincerely yours, Koji 3, 9m 20d [12 October 1557], Masakage

The expression 'we confronted Harunobu and gave battle' certainly implies a major clash between Kenshin and Shingen, but it is more likely that the Takeda main body were nowhere near. Once again, firm details of the conflict are sadly lacking, although a supposed description of the fighting may be found in an account ostensibly about the fifth battle of Kawanakajima, but which may be shown on inspection to refer to Uenohara. It tells us that while the Uesugi troops were having breakfast Shingen made a surprise attack. The Uesugi were driven away after fierce fighting, and the Takeda set fire to their position. The Uesugi then counterattacked, however, and the Takeda withdrew having lost 1,013 men to the Uesugi's 897.

This account is probably inaccurate and is at least greatly exaggerated. Uenohara was by no interpretation a major battle, but rather the endgame of a scenario that had played out from March to September. Kenshin had originally planned to entice Shingen into a decisive battle. Instead of a major clash early in the course of events, six months went by before two tired armies committed themselves to anything like an engagement. Even then there was a palpable hesitancy and reluctance to risk a decisive showdown. They would have to wait another four years for the long-anticipated full-scale battle of Kawanakajima.

THE FOURTH BATTLE OF KAWANAKAJIMA, 1561

The fourth battle of Kawanakajima is often simply referred to as 'the battle of Kawanakajima'. It is the one most usually depicted in works of art and eclipsed in scale any encounter that had preceded it. It was also as bloody a battle as any of the Sengoku Period, a war of attrition that implies an eruption of the frustration that must have been accumulating on both sides over the three indecisive rounds of 1553, 1555 and 1557.

Most descriptions of the battle, which was fought on 18 October 1561, begin with the advance of Shingen and Kenshin into the Kawanakajima area, but these movements did not mark the beginning of the operation but its climax. Just as in each of the three previous encounters, this greatest of all battles of Kawanakajima came after a period of manoeuvring for position and a series of raids and counter-raids. Where the fourth battle differs from the previous three rounds is in the outcome of the encounter at Hachimanbara on the plain of Kawanakajima. This time there was no glaring across a river or a skirmish between vanguard and rearguard. Instead there took place one of the fiercest battles in Japanese history.

Four years went by between the third battle in 1557 and the fourth in 1561. It was a period that saw some momentous changes in the Japanese political scene, most of which seem to have touched Shingen and Kenshin very lightly. The famous battle of Okehazama in 1560, which was to have such resonance in the years to come because of the victory of Oda Nobunaga, caused little alarm up in the Japan Alps, and probably some pleasure as they heard of the death of their rival Imagawa Yoshimoto.

Although Takeda Shingen and Uesugi Kenshin seem to have avoided each other until 1561, they were by no means idle when it came to tackling other rivals, through whom they effectively waged war on each other by proxy. The most significant move occurred in March 1561 when Uesugi Kenshin asserted his newly acquired title of Kanto Kanrei by

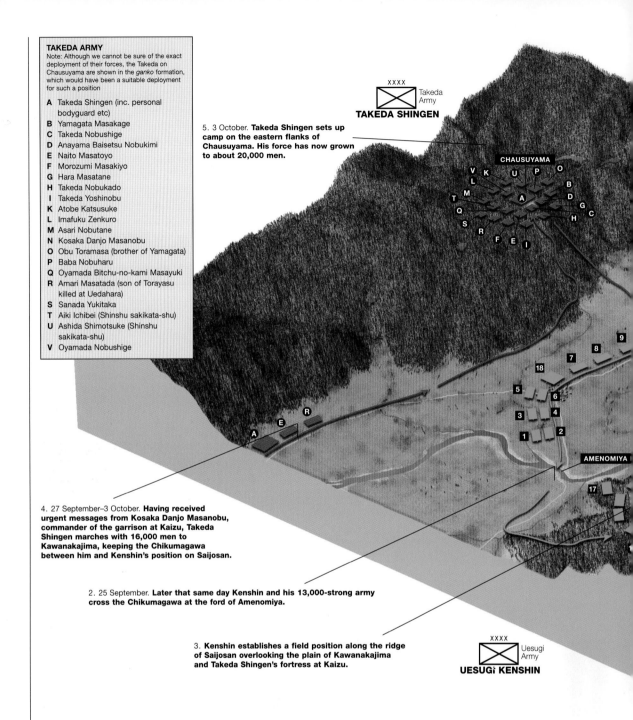

TAKEDA ARMY

Note: Although we cannot be sure of the exact deployment of their forces, the Takeda on Chausuyama are shown in the *ganko* formation, which would have been a suitable deployment for such a position

A   Takeda Shingen (inc. personal bodyguard etc)
B   Yamagata Masakage
C   Takeda Nobushige
D   Anayama Baisetsu Nobukimi
E   Naito Masatoyo
F   Morozumi Masakiyo
G   Hara Masatane
H   Takeda Nobukado
I   Takeda Yoshinobu
K   Atobe Katsusuke
L   Imafuku Zenkuro
M   Asari Nobutane
N   Kosaka Danjo Masanobu
O   Obu Toramasa (brother of Yamagata)
P   Baba Nobuharu
Q   Oyamada Bitchu-no-kami Masayuki
R   Amari Masatada (son of Torayasu killed at Uedahara)
S   Sanada Yukitaka
T   Aiki Ichibei (Shinshu sakikata-shu)
U   Ashida Shimotsuke (Shinshu sakikata-shu)
V   Oyamada Nobushige

XXXX Takeda Army
TAKEDA SHINGEN

5. 3 October. **Takeda Shingen sets up camp on the eastern flanks of Chausuyama. His force has now grown to about 20,000 men.**

CHAUSUYAMA

AMENOMIYA

4. 27 September–3 October. **Having received urgent messages from Kosaka Danjo Masanobu, commander of the garrison at Kaizu, Takeda Shingen marches with 16,000 men to Kawanakajima, keeping the Chikumagawa between him and Kenshin's position on Saijosan.**

2. 25 September. **Later that same day Kenshin and his 13,000-strong army cross the Chikumagawa at the ford of Amenomiya.**

3. **Kenshin establishes a field position along the ridge of Saijosan overlooking the plain of Kawanakajima and Takeda Shingen's fortress at Kaizu.**

XXXX Uesugi Army
UESUGI KENSHIN

FOURTH BATTLE OF KAWANAKAJIMA – THE FIRST PHASE

25 September–8 October 1561, viewed from the southeast. Uesugi Kenshin marches to threaten the fortress of Kaizu to tempt Takeda Shingen into battle. Shingen responds and marches a large army to relieve the fortress.

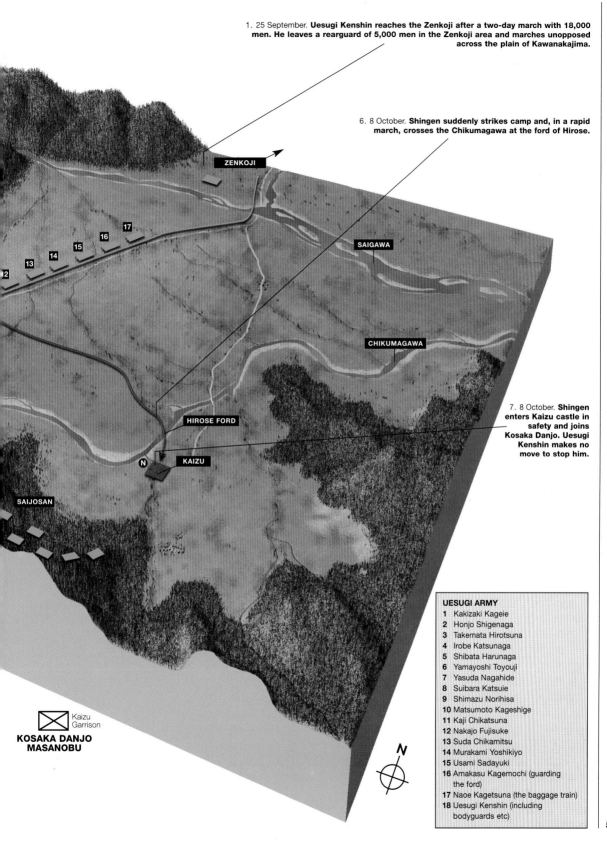

1. 25 September. **Uesugi Kenshin reaches the Zenkoji after a two-day march with 18,000 men. He leaves a rearguard of 5,000 men in the Zenkoji area and marches unopposed across the plain of Kawanakajima.**

6. 8 October. **Shingen suddenly strikes camp and, in a rapid march, crosses the Chikumagawa at the ford of Hirose.**

ZENKOJI

SAIGAWA

CHIKUMAGAWA

7. 8 October. **Shingen enters Kaizu castle in safety and joins Kosaka Danjo. Uesugi Kenshin makes no move to stop him.**

HIROSE FORD

KAIZU

SAIJOSAN

Kaizu Garrison

KOSAKA DANJO MASANOBU

N

UESUGI ARMY
1 Kakizaki Kageie
2 Honjo Shigenaga
3 Takemata Hirotsuna
4 Irobe Katsunaga
5 Shibata Harunaga
6 Yamayoshi Toyouji
7 Yasuda Nagahide
8 Suibara Katsuie
9 Shimazu Norihisa
10 Matsumoto Kageshige
11 Kaji Chikatsuna
12 Nakajo Fujisuke
13 Suda Chikamitsu
14 Murakami Yoshikiyo
15 Usami Sadayuki
16 Amakasu Kagemochi (guarding the ford)
17 Naoe Kagetsuna (the baggage train)
18 Uesugi Kenshin (including bodyguards etc)

A summer view of the highest point of Saijosan viewed from the railway line immediately below. This photograph was taken in 1986, before the building of the motorway. Saijosan allowed the Uesugi to dominate the area from the left flank of Shingen's yamashiro chain. Kenshin strengthened Saijosan with field fortifications

leading an advance against the Hojo and their control of the Kanto. It was the most decisive move made against the Hojo by the Uesugi in over a decade. By advancing to the east of Mount Fuji, Kenshin skirted the Takeda territories to lay siege to the Hojo's mighty castle of Odawara on Sagami Bay. Odawara held out and, when faced by a massive countermove against him, Kenshin withdrew well satisfied by his show of strength.

When Uesugi Kenshin attacked Odawara castle, Takeda Shingen's support for Hojo Ujiyasu took the form of more than just encouraging words. In May 1561 Shingen crossed the Usui Pass into western Kozuke as a defiant demonstration against Kenshin's expansionist pretensions, and in June he made his first move of that year towards northern Shinano. Viewed in the light of the three previous battles, this operation may be justifiably regarded as the opening shot of the fourth battle of Kawanakajima.

It was a raid very similar to the ones carried out in previous years. A detachment of Takeda troops advanced along the Katsurayama/Iizuna route to descend upon and capture the Uesugi-held castle of Warigadake near the shore of Lake Nojiri. Warigadake was very close to the Echigo border, so on 9 August Kenshin began preparations to move to Kawanakajima to repel a possible full-scale invasion of Echigo by a Takeda army.

Although Uesugi Kenshin's greatest fear was an invasion of Echigo over the Togakushi/Iizuna route, he appreciated that to reach those passes a Takeda army would first have to pass through the Kawanakajima area. That was where they could be stopped, so Uesugi Kenshin marched to Kawanakajima on 23 September at the head of 18,000 troops. Allied armies from Iwashiro and Dewa provinces joined him in the form of the Ashina and Daihoji families. Saito Tomonobu and Sambonji Sadanaga were sent to guard against any advance from the direction of Etchu province, thus protecting the Uesugi flanks from a distance. Kenshin's brother-in-law Nagao Masakage was left in charge at Kasugayama.

It is not known for certain which route Kenshin took in 1561, but it is likely that he crossed the Sekida Pass and approached Zenkoji along the western bank of the Chikumagawa, keeping the Chikumagawa between him and Shingen for as much of his journey as possible. This was now a vital consideration, because the strategic situation beside the Chikumagawa was very different from 1557.

The past four years had seen several important changes in the strategic balance around Kawanakajima. Shingen had clearly recalled how, during the second and third campaigns, Kenshin had established positions for himself among the hills around Zenkoji, thus giving himself the protection of three natural moats. By 1561 Takeda Shingen had completed mirror-image preparations on the southern and eastern side of Kawanakajima. He already controlled the castle of Amakazari, which had been captured for him by Sanada Yukitaka in September 1556. In October 1559 he captured Takanashi castle downstream on the eastern bank of the Chikumagawa. Through the seizure of these fortresses the Chikumagawa had become the border between Takeda and Uesugi forces in northern Shinano.

There was also an important addition to Shingen's line of yamashiro, because he had built a new castle on the plain below Amakazari in 1560. This *hirajiro* (a 'plain castle' as distinct from a yamashiro) was called Kaizu. Its ruins now lie within the town of Matsushiro, where it is also called Matsushiro castle. The strategic value of Kaizu is not immediately apparent to a modern visitor because the Chikumagawa has altered its flow in this area. It now bends round much further north than it did in 1561, when it flowed quite close to the castle, which controlled the important ford of Hirose. With Kaizu as a base, a Takeda army could be moved rapidly into the Kawanakajima triangle, thus obviating the need for a field position like the one Shingen had established at Otsuka in 1555.

There was however a further crossing point of the Chikumagawa a short distance upstream at the ford of Amenomiya. This gave closer access to the valley that ran towards Kai, so when Uesugi Kenshin arrived

The ruins of the vitally important 'plain castle' of Kaizu. Although the course of the Chikumagawa has since changed markedly, in 1561 it flowed closer to the castle, which controlled the important ford of Hirose.

at Kawanakajima after his fateful two-day march he headed straight for Amenomiya. He fully appreciated the threat from Kaizu, and resolved to counter it by taking up a field position on a mountain that overlooked his enemy's base.

Leaving 5,000 men as a rearguard in Zenkoji, Kenshin crossed the Susohana, the Sai and the Chikuma rivers on 25 September, rushing across the Amenomiya ford to occupy the hill immediately adjacent to it. The hill, called Saijosan, consisted of a spur projecting northwards like a salient from the central mountain range. In spite of its low elevation (a mere 1,600ft) it allowed the Uesugi to dominate the area from the left flank of Shingen's yamashiro chain. Kenshin strengthened Saijosan with field fortifications, and began to wait patiently for any move from the Kai army.

Takeda Shingen was still in Kofu when Kenshin's rapid advance across the Chikumagawa to Saijosan took place. Kosaka Danjo Masanobu was in charge of Kaizu, and he ensured that the news that Kenshin was on the move soon reached Tsutsujigasaki. Kaizu was 90 miles from Tsutsujigasaki, but the well-organised system of signal fires and mounted messengers enabled Kosaka Danjo to transmit the news that Kenshin had advanced to his lord in less than two hours.

The main source for the tumultuous events of the month that followed is the great epic of the Takeda called *Koyo Gunkan*. Although written several years after the event it is attributed to an eyewitness, and tallies with many of the details contained in letters and reports written by both commanders after the battle. Kenshin's latest change of name from Kagetora to Terutora appears in the narrative. Its account of the fourth battle of Kawanakajima begins with the words:

A signalling beacon as used by the Takeda to communicate across their territories. For example, Kaizu was 90 miles from Tsutsujigasaki, but in 1561 the well-organised system of signal fires and mounted messengers enabled Kosaka Danjo to transmit the news that Kenshin had advanced to his lord in less than two hours.

On the sixteenth day of the eighth month of the fourth year of Eiroku, an express messenger from Kawanakajima in Shinano arrived and reported, 'Terutora has come and is encamped on Saijosan, facing Kaizu castle, and he says that he will make sure he brings down the castle. His army consists of about 13,000 men.'

Uesugi Kenshin made no attempt to prevent the message from getting through. His threat to Kaizu was merely the bait that would encourage Shingen to bring a large army to the foot of Saijosan where Kenshin could fall upon him. It was the Uenohara scenario once again, but played out across the river in Takeda territory.

Takeda Shingen's advance to Kawanakajima, 27 September–8 October 1561

As soon as Shingen received the signal from Kaizu he gave orders for the Kai-based army to mobilise and took personal command of a host of 16,000 men. He left Kofu on 27 September. They marched in two columns via Suwa and Saku, rejoined near Ueda and continued north on the west bank of the Chikumagawa. They arrived in the Kawanakajima area on 3 October. His choice of the west bank is interesting, because even though the route taken placed him across the river from friendly Kaizu it meant that the Chikumagawa stayed between him and Kenshin on Saijosan for the whole journey. The Takeda army pitched camp on the eastern slopes of Chausuyama (2,400ft), thus placing themselves between Kenshin and the Uesugi road home.

Kenshin's men expressed their concern, saying that the retreat route to Echigo was cut off, and that it was like being caught in a bag, but Terutora showed no concern whatsoever.

It was a similar situation to that during the second battle of Kawanakajima when the two evenly balanced armies had faced each other across the Saigawa, and for several days neither army made a move. Both realised that to gain a victory they required the element of surprise to throw their adversary off balance.

Then things started to happen, because on 8 October Shingen suddenly struck camp, marched straight forward under the eyes of the watchers on Saijosan, and crossed the Chikumagawa by the Hirose ford to march directly into Kaizu castle. The numbers of his troops, swollen by reinforcements from Shinano, had now grown to about 20,000 men, but this vast host were not to remain packed into the tiny castle for long. Takeda Shingen, or rather his *gun-bugyo* (army commissioner), Yamamoto Kansuke, had other plans.

Yamamoto Kansuke Haruyuki, to give him his full name, is one of the most interesting of Shingen's generals. He too had taken holy orders, (Kansuke is a Buddhist name, like Shingen) and is frequently represented wearing a white head cowl in place of his spectacular buffalo-horned helmet. Although handicapped by having only one good leg and one good eye, this minor warrior's military talents had long been recognised, and he had been taken into the Takeda army on the personal recommendation of Itagaki Nobukata, who had been killed at Uedahara in 1548. Yamamoto Kansuke had risen to be Shingen's right-hand man, and was nearly 70 years old at Kawanakajima.

It was in his capacity as Shingen's military adviser that he drew up the plans for 'Operation Woodpecker' – a somewhat free translation of the term 'kitsutsuki no sempo', which *Koyo Gunkan* uses for the scheme that would allow the Takeda to launch a surprise attack on the Uesugi. The *kitsutsuki* (woodpecker) strikes its beak on the bark of a tree, and when the insects rush out through the hole in the bark the bird gobbles them up. That was

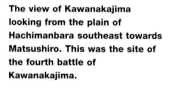

The view of Kawanakajima looking from the plain of Hachimanbara southeast towards Matsushiro. This was the site of the fourth battle of Kawanakajima.

Yamamoto Kansuke's analogy with the pincer attack that he planned.

The strategy was that Takeda Shingen would leave Kaizu at midnight on 17 October with 8,000 men in complete secrecy and in total silence. He would cross the river at Hirose ford on the far side of Kaizu from Saijosan and march to Hachimanbara (the aptly named 'plain of the god of war') in the centre of the flatlands of Kawanakajima to take up a prepared battle formation, all under the cover of darkness. When this had been achieved Kosaka Danjo Masanobu was to play the part of the woodpecker. With a force of 12,000 men he was to climb Saijosan from the rear, again by night and in silence, and attack the Uesugi positions. Kosaka Danjo's assault would drive the Uesugi army down the north side of the mountain, across the Chikumagawa at the ford of Amenomiya and onto the waiting muzzles and blades of Shingen's main body. Kenshin's array would therefore be caught between two samurai armies as dawn broke, and utterly destroyed. It would be a glorious victory, and as Hachimanbara lay midway between the Chikumagawa and the Saigawa the resulting battle would be the first encounter since Fuse in 1553 to fully deserve the title of the battle of Kawanakajima.

Yamamoto Kansuke, who devised Operation Woodpecker, shown prepared to die to atone for his mistake. Kansuke, like Shingen, had taken holy orders and is frequently shown wearing a white head cowl rather than his spectacular buffalo-horned helmet.

Kansuke said, 'Out of your 20,000 men, my lord, 12,000 should be sent against Kenshin's camp on Saijosan to begin an attack at about the Hour of the Hare tomorrow. Whether or not the Echigo force win or lose this encounter, they are bound to retreat across the river. When they do so the units led by your close retainers and the men of the two reserves will attack them from the rear and finish them off.'

Of all the battles of Kawanakajima only the fourth provides us with enough information to make a reliable statement about the numbers and names of the men engaged on each side. Takeda Shingen is said to have crossed the Chikumagawa with 8,000 men while 12,000 attacked Saijosan from the rear. This implies that almost no one was left in Kaizu castle, which is somewhat surprising, but *Koyo Gunkan* is quite precise about the named individuals present at the encounter.

To the names that follow I have added the numbers of horsemen noted for each individual (or his son) in the list of 1573, exactly as I did in my Campaign Series book *Nagashino 1575 – Slaughter at the barricades*. The rest of the 8,000-strong army would be made up by the mounted samurai's attendants (at two each per man) and ashigaru. So, for example,

Takeda Nobushige's personal command is estimated as 200 horsemen (the number credited to his son Nobutoyo in 1573), while the chronicles state his total command at Kawanakajima as 700 men. This allows for 500 other troops. Takeda Shingen's force was therefore as follows:

Yamagata Masakage	300
Takeda Nobushige	200
Anayama Baisetsu Nobukimi	200
Naito Masatoyo	250
Morozumi Masakiyo	not listed
Hara Masatane	120
Takeda Nobukado	80
Takeda Yoshinobu	200 (estimated)
Mochizuki Masayori	60
Atobe Katsusuke	300
Imafuku Zenkuro	70
Asari Nobutane	120

The Saijosan force consisted of the following commanders and their horsemen, plus attendants and ashigaru:

Kosaka Danjo Masanobu	450
Obu Toramasa (brother of Yamagata)	not listed
Baba Nobuharu	120
Oyamada Bitchu-no-kami Masayuki	70
Amari Masatada (son of Torayasu killed at Uedahara)	100
Sanada Yukitaka	200
Aiki Ichibei (Shinshu sakikata-shu)	80
Ashida Shimotsuke (Shinshu sakikata-shu)	150
Oyamada Nobushige	200
Obata Masamori (son of the late Toramori)	not listed

The accepted figures for the Uesugi army are that Kenshin left Kasugayama castle with 18,000 men, of whom 5,000 were left as a rearguard in Zenkoji while 13,000 proceeded to Saijosan, all of whom were apparently deployed for the battle. Amakasu Kagemochi stayed at the ford with 1,000 men and Naoe Kagetsuna guarded the baggage train with 2,000 men. This leaves 10,000 for Kenshin's dawn attack, but when we come to the fine detail of the names involved our sources are less precise than the Takeda and are often contradictory. We can say for certain that Saito Tomonobu, Sambonji Sadanaga and Nagao Masakage were not at Kawanakajima. Some of the other big names in the Uesugi army no doubt stayed at Zenkoji, but sources do not tell us who these men were. However, we can say with confidence that the following Uesugi generals took part in the battle because their names appear in the chronicles or are 'mentioned in dispatches'. Unfortunately it is not possible to list the individual contributions from each general without being very misleading, because the only available source of figures dates from the above mentioned document of 1575, and the numbers do not tally as well as the Takeda figures do. So for example Kakizaki Kageie, who led the vanguard of 1,500 men at Kawanakajima, is listed in the 1575 register as supplying 260 men in total, of whom only 20 are mounted samurai. The names of the known Uesugi generals are:

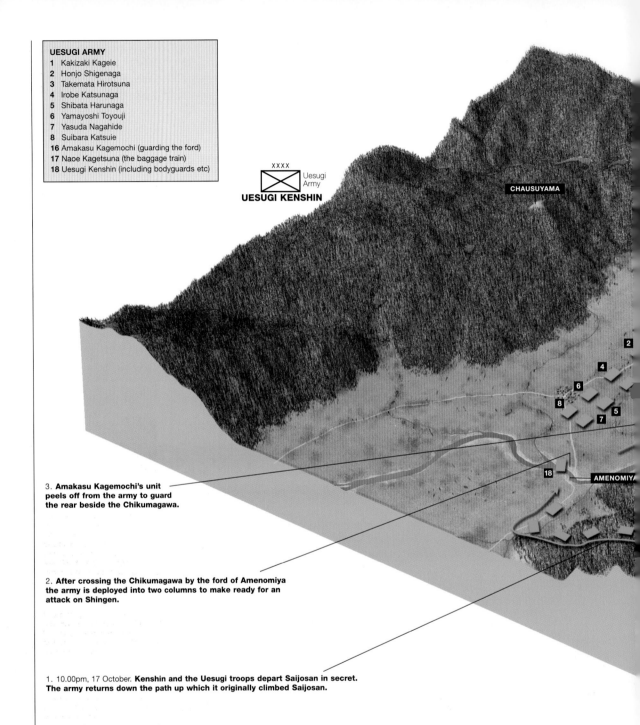

UESUGI ARMY
1 Kakizaki Kageie
2 Honjo Shigenaga
3 Takemata Hirotsuna
4 Irobe Katsunaga
5 Shibata Harunaga
6 Yamayoshi Toyouji
7 Yasuda Nagahide
8 Suibara Katsuie
16 Amakasu Kagemochi (guarding the ford)
17 Naoe Kagetsuna (the baggage train)
18 Uesugi Kenshin (including bodyguards etc)

xxxx
Uesugi Army
UESUGI KENSHIN

CHAUSUYAMA

AMENOMIYA

3. **Amakasu Kagemochi's unit peels off from the army to guard the rear beside the Chikumagawa.**

2. **After crossing the Chikumagawa by the ford of Amenomiya the army is deployed into two columns to make ready for an attack on Shingen.**

1. 10.00pm, 17 October. **Kenshin and the Uesugi troops depart Saijosan in secret. The army returns down the path up which it originally climbed Saijosan.**

FOURTH BATTLE OF KAWANAKAJIMA – THE NIGHT MANOEUVRES

17/18 October 1561, 10.00pm–12.00am, viewed from the southeast. Takeda Shingen redeploys his troops in preparation for a surprise dawn attack on the Uesugi aimed at destroying Kenshin's army. What he does not know is that the Uesugi are also on the move – down onto the plain of Kawanakajima.

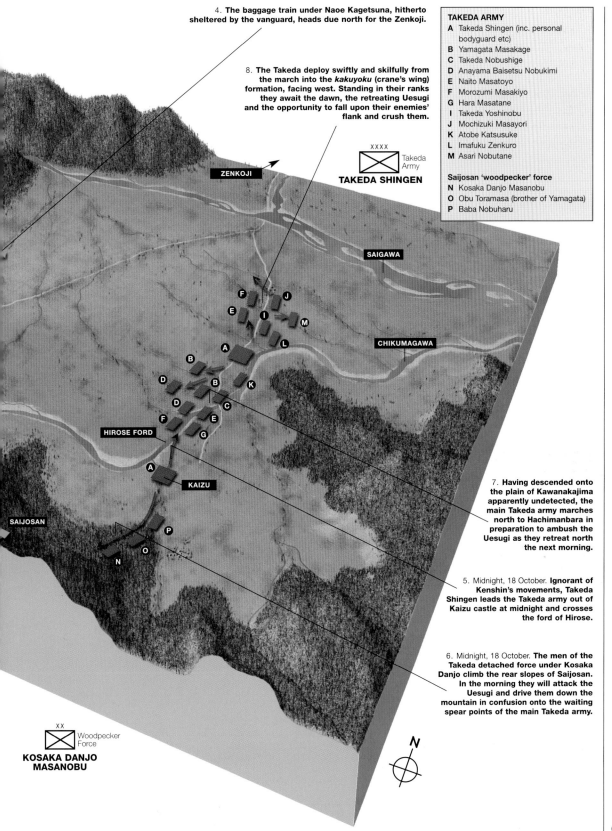

4. The baggage train under Naoe Kagetsuna, hitherto sheltered by the vanguard, heads due north for the Zenkoji.

8. The Takeda deploy swiftly and skilfully from the march into the *kakuyoku* (crane's wing) formation, facing west. Standing in their ranks they await the dawn, the retreating Uesugi and the opportunity to fall upon their enemies' flank and crush them.

xxxx

Takeda Army

TAKEDA SHINGEN

ZENKOJI

SAIGAWA

CHIKUMAGAWA

HIROSE FORD

KAIZU

SAIJOSAN

TAKEDA ARMY
- A Takeda Shingen (inc. personal bodyguard etc)
- B Yamagata Masakage
- C Takeda Nobushige
- D Anayama Baisetsu Nobukimi
- E Naito Masatoyo
- F Morozumi Masakiyo
- G Hara Masatane
- I Takeda Yoshinobu
- J Mochizuki Masayori
- K Atobe Katsusuke
- L Imafuku Zenkuro
- M Asari Nobutane

Saijosan 'woodpecker' force
- N Kosaka Danjo Masanobu
- O Obu Toramasa (brother of Yamagata)
- P Baba Nobuharu

7. Having descended onto the plain of Kawanakajima apparently undetected, the main Takeda army marches north to Hachimanbara in preparation to ambush the Uesugi as they retreat north the next morning.

5. Midnight, 18 October. Ignorant of Kenshin's movements, Takeda Shingen leads the Takeda army out of Kaizu castle at midnight and crosses the ford of Hirose.

6. Midnight, 18 October. The men of the Takeda detached force under Kosaka Danjo climb the rear slopes of Saijosan. In the morning they will attack the Uesugi and drive them down the mountain in confusion onto the waiting spear points of the main Takeda army.

xx

Woodpecker Force

KOSAKA DANJO MASANOBU

N

Kakizaki Kageie
Honjo Shigenaga
Takemata Hirotsuna
Irobe Katsunaga
Shibata Harunaga
Yamayoshi Toyouji
Yasuda Nagahide
Suibara Katsuie
Shimazu Norihisa
Matsumoto Kageshige
Kaji Chikatsuna
Nakajo Fujisuke
Suda Chikamitsu
Murakami Yoshikiyo
Usami Sadayuki
Amakasu Kagemochi (guarding the ford)
Naoe Kagetsuna (the baggage train)

Uesugi Kenshin had a war band known popularly as the 'Seventeen Generals' or the 'Twenty-Eight Generals'. This is Kakizaki Kageie, who led the Uesugi advance at the fourth battle of Kawanakajima.

As the Uesugi battle array was probably two advancing columns their actual positions during the battle can only be inferred from descriptions, but a likely scenario is indicated in the accompanying bird's-eye view.

Operation Woodpecker

Operation Woodpecker began as Yamamoto had planned at midnight. Takeda Shingen led 8,000 men out of Kaizu across the Chikumagawa to Hachimanbara, which would have involved a short march of about two and a half miles. Here, according to *Koyo Gunkan*, he drew up his army, which covered an area of about 1,500 square yards, in the battle formation known as *kakuyoku* (crane's wing). The old chronicles are very fond of describing battle formations in such poetic language, giving certain formations names that would be understandable to the samurai clientele for whom these epics were written. A series of set battle formations based on Chinese originals is implied, and it is more than likely that both Shingen and Kenshin had great skills in arranging these tried and tested formations. The mere fact that the Takeda arrangement was carried out in almost total darkness suggests that hours must have been spent training the Takeda army to move quickly into pre-arranged positions.

So the Takeda formed their 8,000-man kakuyoku, which the distinguished military historian Sasama tells us is the best formation for surrounding an advancing enemy. It has the appearance of a shallow formation like the swept-back wings of a crane. The headquarters unit lies behind the wings, and there is a rearguard. On Hachimanbara the vanguard units were Yamagata Masakage, Takeda Nobushige (Shingen's brother) and Naito Masatoyo, with Morozumi Masakiyo (Shingen's uncle) and Anayama Nobukimi as right and left 'wingtips'. Behind them was Shingen's main body with Hara Masatane and Takeda Nobukado (Shingen's brother) on the left, Mochizuki Masayori (his nephew) and Takeda Yoshinobu (Shingen's son and heir) on the right, although descriptions of the battle suggest that all these four units were pushed forward into the crane's wing when the fighting started. Atobe Katsusuke, Imafuku Zenkuro and Asari Nobutane provided a rearguard.

Shingen's *maku*, the cloth curtains ornamented with the Takeda mon, or badge, were set up to form his headquarters post in the centre of his army. Here he sat, waiting for the dawn and hundreds of fleeing Uesugi samurai to approach the kakuyoku. But when dawn came there was no sign of any fugitives. Something had gone seriously wrong.

Unknown to Shingen, Uesugi Kenshin was not entirely ignorant of his plans and had not been idle. His scouts on Saijosan, or perhaps vigilant spies sent down to Kaizu castle, reported seeing clear signs that Shingen was making a move. Kenshin guessed what the plan might be and planned a countermove, also to be carried out at dead of night. *Koyo Gunkan*, although heavily biased towards the Takeda, credits Kenshin with commendable strategic foresight. It nevertheless begins by putting into Kenshin's mouth a passage of suitable self-deprecation:

Fifteen years ago in the Year of the Ram when Shingen was 27 and I was 18 we began our struggle. Since then we have engaged in battle on several occasions. But every time Shingen was careful not to make any mistakes over his deployment and in the end he gave the impression that he dominated the battlefield with me as the loser. Now I see that he is preparing for battle tomorrow. And what I see as clearly as if it were reflected in a mirror is this. His strategy is to divide his men into two divisions. One will come over to this position to begin the battle. The other will finish off my hatamoto as they cross the river to withdraw.

Let us outwit him just this once. We will cross the river ourselves and spend the night there. As the sun rises we will attack Shingen's army to start a battle, and will throw them back before his vanguard even manage to reach us. We will ensure that Shingen's hatamoto fight with mine. Why, Shingen and I may even fight each other in single combat to stab each other to death. If that is not possible, we will agree a truce. Either way, tomorrow's battle will be a once in a lifetime experience!

It would appear that Kenshin began his daring pre-emptive move before Shingen had moved even a single ashigaru out of Kaizu. Uesugi

The grave of Takeda Nobushige lies close to where he fell at the fourth battle of Kawanakajima.

TAKEMATA HIROTSUNA AT HACHIMANBARA, 1561
(pages 70–71)

The fourth battle of Kawanakajima opened with a ferocious Uesugi charge against the Takeda lines. The first wave was commanded by Kakizaki Kageie (1) whose banner bears the device of a grasshopper (2). His troops are identified by the *mon* (badge) of a giant radish on their sashimono flags (3). Having made the initial attack, Kakizaki Kageie's men are falling back to reorganise. Attacking into the sun has not deterred the Uesugi from attempting to destroy the Takeda with a series of cavalry charges supported by dismounted troops. Now the second wave of Uesugi troops, commanded by Takemata Hirotsuna (4), sweep forwards. Like all senior commanders, he is identified by his standard, which is a three-dimensional golden bamboo screen like a Venetian blind (5). His followers wear a white sashimono with a black ring (6). In a dramatic incident recounted in the *Koyo Gunkan*, on reaching the Takeda lines Hirotsuna has been knocked off his horse with such force that his helmet has been dislodged from his head. He wears a rather old-fashioned *do-maru*

style of armour (7) with close spaced *kebiki*-style lacing on the plates. Behind him other Uesugi samurai press home their own attacks. Suda Chikamitsu leads forward his ashigaru (8) who wear a *mon* of a gold swastika on blue. They wear straw sandals below their modern-style shin guards (9) consisting of narrow iron strips on a cloth backing. Behind them can be seen the troops of Suibara Katsuie, with their banners of a white crescent on a red field (10), and further back Matsumoto Kageshige's men with their black and white sashimono (11). The Takeda troops facing the charge included those of Naito Masatoyo who wear black and white flags (12), although other sources state their flags were red and white. They stand alongside the troops of Takeda Shingen's uncle, Morozumi Masakiyo, with their black on blue Takeda sashimono (13). Morozumi Masakiyo commanded the right 'wing tip' of the Takeda *kakuyoku* (crane's wing) formation and was killed during the battle. The surprise Uesugi attacks won them a considerable initial advantage and they succeeded in breaking through as far Takeda Shingen's curtained headquarters. (Wayne Reynolds)

Kenshin had in fact descended from Saijosan by rough mountain paths in total secrecy at about 10.00pm on 17 October. So instead of fleeing before Kosaka Danjo's dawn attack the Uesugi army had already crept carefully down the mountain the night before. To deaden the noise of movement his horses hooves and bits were padded with cloth:

> As he did so not a sound was heard even though there were as many as 13,000 men. This was because according to orders issued in their camp that breakfast time each Echigo man had been told to prepare enough food for three men. They therefore had no need to cook food for the evening meal, so there was no sign of fires being made.

This passage is rather difficult to understand, because an absence of cooking fires on Saijosan that evening would surely have sent the opposite message to Shingen and given the game away. Kenshin may well have left some men on Saijosan to give an impression of normality, so the passage probably means that the army cooked extra food at breakfast time for the following day while the evening meal looked perfectly normal.

Takeda Shingen's approach to Hachimanbara from Kaizu involved no descent of a mountain, just a straight march and a wading of the river, and at first sight it seems extraordinary that Shingen had not sent out scouts towards Amenomiya. If he had done so Kenshin's army would undoubtedly have been spotted. The probable reason why Shingen did not send out scouts was that he assumed that Kenshin's army was sitting on Saijosan in blissful ignorance of his own crossing, and he dared do nothing that would arose their suspicions. The result was that two armies took up battle positions in pitch darkness, with the Takeda being so discreet that they had no idea that the other was there!

We must now ask ourselves in which direction the Takeda army was facing. A glance at the map shows that it must have been west. Shingen would have reasoned that after crossing the Chikumagawa by the ford of Amenomiya the fleeing and panic-stricken Uesugi army would have swung round to the northwest for the safety of the Zenkoji and the natural moats of the Saigawa and Susohanagawa. The Takeda army would have the rising sun behind them, and as they advanced to take the disorganised Uesugi army in their right flank their enemies would turn and be dazzled both by the sun and the unexpected Takeda attack. But as dawn broke the Takeda army peered through the dispersing mist to find the Uesugi army not fleeing across their front but bearing down upon them in a fierce head-on charge.

Kenshin's dawn attack

Takeda Nobushige on the left wing of the vanguard received the initial shock of the Uesugi surprise attack. In the words of the poet Rai San'yo, in an action he calls romantically 'a whip crack across the river', dawn broke to reveal 'a thousand horsemen advancing with the break of day'. Kenshin ordered his men to lower their heads and not look at the enemy so that their helmets and neckguards would protect them against arrows and bullets. Kenshin shouted, 'Ei! Ei!' to which his samurai replied with, 'O! O!' and in they charged.

The surprise caused by Kenshin's attack should not imply that his advance was a reckless charge. The descent of the mountain paths and the crossing of the ford would inevitably have placed his army into temporary disorder, but it was speedily corrected. A well-ordered advance may therefore be envisaged. The bulk of the Uesugi army marched on into the darkness in the general direction of Zenkoji while Amakasu Kagemochi was left behind to guard the ford of Amenomiya with 1,000 men. The only other unit that was not expected to go directly into action against Shingen was the baggage train guarded by 2,000 men under Naoe Kagetsuna, who headed directly for the fords of the Saigawa and the safe haven of Zenkoji. We may envisage this unit being protected by the other columns until they 'peeled off' to attack Shingen's newly discovered position, keeping the baggage always to their rear.

The vanguard commander, Kakizaki Kageie, led the Uesugi attack on Takeda Nobushige with 1,500 men. His unit of mounted samurai, who proudly flew a sashimono flag of a giant radish, crashed into the Takeda unit. Nobushige died in the fierce hand-to-hand fighting that followed. As Kakizaki's unit withdrew to rest they were replaced by fresh bands of mounted samurai who kept up the pressure. Takemata Hirotsuna next led his followers against the veteran Takeda leaders Naito Masatoyo and Morozumi Masakiyo on the right wing, and was knocked clean off his horse, the force of the blow as he hit the ground dislodging his helmet. Once again the Uesugi tactic of rotating the front-line troops was put into operation, and Takemata Hirotsuna withdrew to be replaced by another.

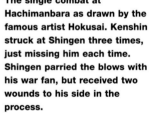

The single combat at Hachimanbara as drawn by the famous artist Hokusai. Kenshin struck at Shingen three times, just missing him each time. Shingen parried the blows with his war fan, but received two wounds to his side in the process.

The single combat at Kawanakajima, as seen in a woodblock print. Kenshin charges in from the right. Shingen's retainers lift their spears to defend him, while Shingen raises his war fan.

Takeda Shingen is shown here with his war fan from the statue group at Hachimanbara, the site of the fourth battle of Kawanakajima.

Uesugi Kenshin striking down with his sword, from the statue group at Hachimanbara.

Uesugi Kenshin's method of rotating his troops is recorded in *Koyo Gunkan* as a set battle formation known as *kuruma gakari*, or 'winding wheel', an expression that has given rise to a great deal of speculation. Various fanciful geometric models have been suggested to show how Kenshin's army was rotated like a huge water wheel, depositing one unit after another against Shingen's front line. Such an elaborate explanation is both unlikely and unnecessary. What probably happened was that after crossing at Amenomiya Kenshin's army marched north in two columns, ready to engage the enemy wherever he might be found. When Shingen's army was discovered (no doubt by mounted scouts) to be lying to the front of their right flank, Kenshin began wheeling his troops for the assault. If he wheeled successive units in turn and replaced one unit by the unit behind them, then the overall exercise would have given the impression of a giant wheel turning.

Meanwhile Takeda Shingen, seated on his folding camp stool, was trying desperately to control his harassed army from his command post within the field curtains. By the good offices of his mounted messengers full communication was maintained with his officers:

Almost at once one unit of Kenshin's hatamoto wheeled round on to the right wing of Shingen's position, drove off Yoshinobu's fifty mounted hatamoto, along with about 400 other soldiers and cut into Shingen's own hatamoto. Three thousand six hundred or three thousand seven hundred soldiers, friends and foes combined, were thrown into the melee stabbing and being stabbed, slashing and being slashed, some grabbing each other's armoured shoulders, grappling and falling down. One would take his enemy's head and rise to his feet only for someone to shout, 'That's my lord's head!' and skewer him with his spear. A third man seeing it would then cut that man down.

The single combat at Takeda Shingen's command post

Great danger was at hand. The enemy had by now reached the Takeda headquarters troops and Shingen's personal bodyguard. Shingen's son Takeda Yoshinobu had been wounded, but at this point there occurred one of the most famous instances of single combat in samurai history. According to *Koyo Gunkan* (the only written source for this celebrated incident) there came bursting into the curtained enclosure a single mounted samurai wearing a white headcowl, and with a green *kataginu* (a form of *jinbaori* or surcoat) over his armour. The figure is believed to have been Uesugi Kenshin himself. He swung his sword at Shingen, who did not have time to draw his own sword. He rose from his camp stool and parried the blows as best he could with the heavy war fan that he had been using for signalling. Kenshin:

struck at him three times, just missing him each time as Shingen stopped the blows with his war fan, but he received two wounds to his side. His chief retainer and the head of the twenty-man bodyguard, each a brave warrior, fought back furiously while keeping him surrounded in case friend or foe should spot him, cutting down anyone who came near.

Hara Osumi-no-kami, one of Shingen's retainers, came to his aid and attacked the horseman with Shingen's own spear with its shaft inlaid

The single combat at Hachimanbara as shown in a woodblock print. This was one of the most famous instances of single combat in samurai history. We see Kenshin cutting into Shingen's war fan with his sword.

with mother-of-pearl, which we may assume Hara was already carrying. The blade glanced off the *watagami* (armpit protectors) of Kenshin's armour, making the spear shaft strike the horse's rump. This caused the beast to rear and bolt. By now others of Shingen's guard had rallied to their master's side, and Kenshin was driven off.

A fine modern statue depicting the fight between the two generals now marks the site of this famous skirmish. Their combat is often depicted in woodblock prints, where Kenshin is usually shown with his horse knocking to one side the curtains and wooden shields that surround the startled Shingen. There is however an alternative tradition that it was not Uesugi Kenshin who fought the combat but one of his vanguard, a samurai by the name of Arakawa. Another samurai called Kojima Yataro appears on some prints joining in the Uesugi attack. Two others of the Uesugi 'Twenty-Eight Generals', Nakajo Fujisuke and Irobe Katsunaga, were also to be later honoured by Kenshin for the part they played in the breakthrough to Shingen's headquarters.

As the wheel wound on Yamamoto Kansuke realised that his carefully made plans had failed. He accepted full responsibility for the disaster that his error of judgement had brought upon them, and resolved to make amends by dying like a true samurai. Taking a long spear in his hands he charged alone into the midst of the Uesugi samurai, where he fought fiercely until, overcome by bullet wounds and arrows, and wounded in 80 places on his body, he retired to a grassy knoll and committed hara kiri.

One by one the Takeda samurai fell. Shingen's brother and Yamamoto Kansuke were followed in death by his uncle Morozumi Bungo-no-kami Masakiyo, who had faced the first assault. Yet in spite of the fierce rotating attacks by the Uesugi army the Takeda main body held firm. Yamagata Masakage fought back against Kakizaki Kageie's samurai. Anayama Baisetsu Nobukimi destroyed Shibata Harunaga and actually succeeded in forcing some of the Uesugi army back towards the Chikumagawa.

The single combat between Kenshin and Shingen is re-enacted at Yonezawa during the 1999 festival. The chronicle tells how there came bursting into the curtained enclosure a single mounted samurai wearing a white headcowl, and with a green *kataginu* (a form of surcoat) over his armour. The figure is believed to have been Uesugi Kenshin himself.

In this print Kojima Yataro (shown top left) helps Kenshin after the single combat against Shingen has ended in failure.

Takeda Nobushige, killed at the fourth battle of Kawanakajima, is shown to the rear of this picture. Takeda Shingen dominates the foreground.

Among Shingen's hatamoto Obu Saburo [Yamagata Masakage] along with his men repelled Echigo's leading troops under Kakizaki and pursued them for about 300 yards. Anayama and his followers too pursued Kenshin's retainer Shibata for about 400 yards. All that time Shingen had only his chief retainers, his twenty-man bodyguard and seventeen of eighteen pages. Tsuchiya Heihachi and Naoda Kihei were among them, and would not draw back one single step, standing at the spot where he rose from his camp stool.

Kosaka Danjo's counterattack

While this surprise attack was going on the 'woodpecker force' under Kosaka Danjo Masanobu had arrived on the summit of Saijosan. Their advance had been conducted in great stealth, and no doubt the silence that greeted them on arriving on the summit was put down to their skill in failing to attract the attention of Kenshin's sentries. They soon realised what had actually happened. The Uesugi position was deserted, and they could hear the noise of battle coming from the plain to the north. So the Takeda force immediately descended from Saijosan by the paths that led down to the ford of Amenomiya.

This was the same route that they had planned should be the one that Kenshin would choose in panic. Instead the detached Takeda force flew down to the ford to hurry to the aid of Shingen's main body. But Uesugi Kenshin had prudently left the ford guarded by 1,000 men under Amakasu Kagemochi. Here took place possibly the most desperate fighting of the day, with victory going eventually to the Takeda. When Kosaka and his men forced their way across the ford the stage was set to reverse all Kenshin's triumphs.

The Takeda detached force poured across the river against the rear of the Uesugi samurai, who were now caught between the arms of the pincers, just as the late Yamamoto Kansuke had planned. It was too late to save the life of Shingen's veteran strategist, but there was still time to save his reputation.

Most people had concluded that Shingen had lost the battle, but when the ten leading commanders who had gone to Saijosan and realised that they had been fooled by Kenshin heard the gunshots and the cries of battle, they vied with one another in crossing the Chikumagawa, and began attacking the Echigo forces from the rear and charged in as soon as the latter withdrew.

The Takeda soon re-established control. A group of soldiers managed to recover from the Uesugi trophy hunters the heads of Shingen's brother Takeda Tenkyu Nobushige and uncle Morozumi Masakiyo:

One of Shingen's warriors, Yamadera by name, regained Tenkyu's head from the man who had taken it and in so doing killed him and brought back that man's head along with Tenkyu's. As for Morozumi, a warrior under his command called Ishiguro Goro and a ronin from Mikawa province called Naruse regained his head and came back with the heads of some Echigo men.

By midday a certain defeat had been turned into something of a victory. The Takeda side counted 3,117 enemy heads taken, and Shingen

THE BATTLE AT THE FORD OF THE CHIKUMAGAWA BESIDE SAIJOSAN, 1561 (pages 78–79)

The surprise attack that was the lynchpin of Yamamoto Kansuke's 'Operation Woodpecker' has been launched against the Uesugi camp on Saijosan but to their horror, the Takeda troops have found the camp deserted. With the sounds of battle drifting up from the plain below, the Takeda have led their horses hurriedly down the mountain path and speedily mounted up for a charge. Uesugi Kenshin has left Amakasu Kagemochi (1) to guard the area of ford across the Chikumagawa directly below the shortest route down from Saijosan. He wears an *okegawa-do* style armour with a solid breastplate and separate plates with *sugake* (spaced out) lacing. The addition of patterned leather makes it more elaborate than that of his followers. His standard, a giant golden three-dimensional sunburst made of lacquered wood (2), is carried by an ashigaru standard bearer (3) who uses a leather bucket at his waist to support the unwieldy device. Amakasu Kagemochi's samurai and ashigaru, with their black and white zigzag flags (4), wear simple 'munitions' armour of straightforward *okegawa-do* styles. They are now facing a furious assault across the river by Shingen's army under Kosaka Danjo Masanobu (5), wearing a facemask and

identified by his yellow flag with a black 'stars' device (6). He was Takeda Shingen's favourite, and is now desperate to lead the army to Hachimanbara to help his lord. Bearing down on Kagemochi, however, are the samurai of Obu Toramasa's 'red regiment', whose use of red-lacquered armour (7) provided the first example of such lavish uniform colour in Japanese history. All the armour and the flags are in the red of victory. The better-known Ii family later copied the dramatic and unmistakable symbolism of the red armour. Their red sashimono have a crescent and disc device in white (8), which is repeated on helmet crests and breast-plates of Obu Toramasa's samurai. As befits a general, Obu Toramasa (9) dresses slightly differently from his men, with a blue and red armour worn under a gold brocade *jinbaori* (surcoat). Men and horses kick up huge splashes as they cross the river. Almost invisible behind them are the samurai of Baba Nobuharu, victor of the siege of Katsurayama castle (10), while streams of Takeda samurai, their sashimono just catching the rays of the sun, follow them down the mountain path out of the morning mist from the wooded slopes of Saijosan (11). This spectacular counter-attack eventually overcame the guards at the ford and sped to Shingen's assistance, saving the day for the Takeda. (Wayne Reynolds)

This view shows the scene of most crucial moment in the fourth battle of Kawanakajima. The detached Takeda force flew down to the paths from Saijosan to hurry to the aid of Shingen's main body. Uesugi Kenshin had left 1,000 men under Amakasu Kagemochi to guard the ford. Amid desperate fighting the Takeda eventually forced their way across. The path follows the top of the triangular section sliced off Saijosan for the motorway. In 1561 the Chikumagawa flowed nearer to the mountain than it does today.

The death of Morozumi Masakiyo, Takeda Shingen's uncle, who committed suicide after being mortally wounded at the fourth battle of Kawanakajima. The artist has shown him wounded by an explosive device, although there are no records of gunpowder weapons of this type being used at Kawanakajima.

held a triumphant head-viewing ceremony, clutching in his hand, one presumes, the battered war fan that had saved his life. Uesugi Kenshin may well have done the same after the bloodiest draw in Japanese history.

The immediate aftermath

On the morning of the following day, a time of truce, Uesugi Kenshin sent three of his generals, Naoe, Amakasu and Usami Sadayuki, to burn what remained of their encampment on Saijosan. It would appear that Takeda Shingen made no attempt to stop them or to interfere with Kenshin's subsequent withdrawal beyond the Saigawa to the Zenkoji. A few days later the retreat took them back to Kasugayama.

The Takeda army was in no better shape than their opponents. On the assumption that the 3,117 heads that were taken by the Takeda only belonged to samurai, the author of the booklet produced by the Kawanakajima battlefield museum estimates that the Uesugi had suffered 72 per cent casualties. He also states that the Takeda, the supposed victors, lost 62 per cent including several of their most able leaders. Even if we take a percentage of Uesugi heads from the figure of 11,000 men, which is the total Uesugi army less Naoe's baggage guard (who appear to have been untouched) the figure is 28 per cent dead. This is a figure that would give any commander some concern, so there is no doubt that the loss of life was heavy.

The fourth battle of Kawanakajima was one of the most extraordinary encounters in 16th-century Japan. The whole strategy of Operation Woodpecker depended upon the absolute secrecy of the crossing of the Hirose ford, but it is strange that no attempt was made by the Takeda to ascertain

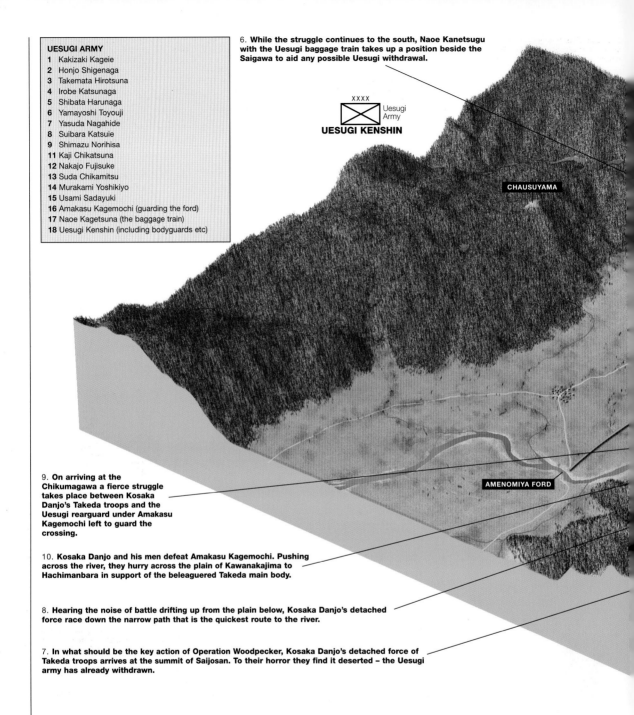

UESUGI ARMY
1 Kakizaki Kageie
2 Honjo Shigenaga
3 Takemata Hirotsuna
4 Irobe Katsunaga
5 Shibata Harunaga
6 Yamayoshi Toyouji
7 Yasuda Nagahide
8 Suibara Katsuie
9 Shimazu Norihisa
11 Kaji Chikatsuna
12 Nakajo Fujisuke
13 Suda Chikamitsu
14 Murakami Yoshikiyo
15 Usami Sadayuki
16 Amakasu Kagemochi (guarding the ford)
17 Naoe Kagetsuna (the baggage train)
18 Uesugi Kenshin (including bodyguards etc)

6. **While the struggle continues to the south, Naoe Kanetsugu with the Uesugi baggage train takes up a position beside the Saigawa to aid any possible Uesugi withdrawal.**

xxxx
Uesugi
Army
UESUGI KENSHIN

CHAUSUYAMA

AMENOMIYA FORD

9. **On arriving at the Chikumagawa a fierce struggle takes place between Kosaka Danjo's Takeda troops and the Uesugi rearguard under Amakasu Kagemochi left to guard the crossing.**

10. **Kosaka Danjo and his men defeat Amakasu Kagemochi. Pushing across the river, they hurry across the plain of Kawanakajima to Hachimanbara in support of the beleaguered Takeda main body.**

8. **Hearing the noise of battle drifting up from the plain below, Kosaka Danjo's detached force race down the narrow path that is the quickest route to the river.**

7. **In what should be the key action of Operation Woodpecker, Kosaka Danjo's detached force of Takeda troops arrives at the summit of Saijosan. To their horror they find it deserted – the Uesugi army has already withdrawn.**

FOURTH BATTLE OF KAWANAKAJIMA – THE CLIMAX OF THE BATTLE

18 October 1561, 6.00am–12.00pm, viewed from the southeast. The Uesugi launch a thundering dawn attack on the Takeda lines as Shingen realises his plans have gone badly awry. Reaching the summit of Saijosan, Kosaka Danjo finds it deserted. Hearing the sounds of battle from the valley below, his men race down the mountain to the aid of their comrades.

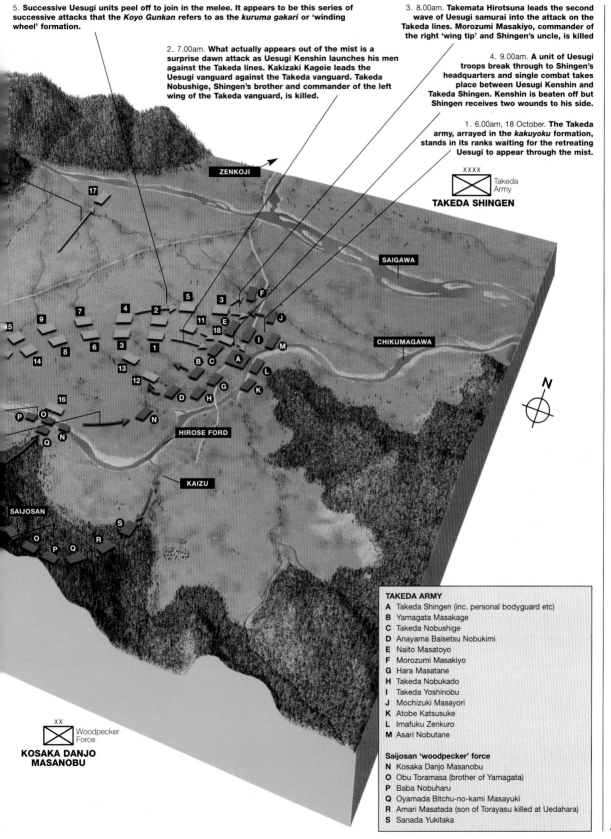

5. Successive Uesugi units peel off to join in the melee. It appears to be this series of successive attacks that the *Koyo Gunkan* refers to as the *kuruma gakari* or 'winding wheel' formation.

2. 7.00am. What actually appears out of the mist is a surprise dawn attack as Uesugi Kenshin launches his men against the Takeda lines. Kakizaki Kageie leads the Uesugi vanguard against the Takeda vanguard. Takeda Nobushige, Shingen's brother and commander of the left wing of the Takeda vanguard, is killed.

3. 8.00am. Takemata Hirotsuna leads the second wave of Uesugi samurai into the attack on the Takeda lines. Morozumi Masakiyo, commander of the right 'wing tip' and Shingen's uncle, is killed

4. 9.00am. A unit of Uesugi troops break through to Shingen's headquarters and single combat takes place between Uesugi Kenshin and Takeda Shingen. Kenshin is beaten off but Shingen receives two wounds to his side.

1. 6.00am, 18 October. The Takeda army, arrayed in the *kakuyoku* formation, stands in its ranks waiting for the retreating Uesugi to appear through the mist.

xxxx
Takeda Army
TAKEDA SHINGEN

ZENKOJI

SAIGAWA

CHIKUMAGAWA

N

HIROSE FORD

KAIZU

SAIJOSAN

xx
Woodpecker Force
KOSAKA DANJO MASANOBU

TAKEDA ARMY
A Takeda Shingen (inc. personal bodyguard etc)
B Yamagata Masakage
C Takeda Nobushige
D Anayama Baisetsu Nobukimi
E Naito Masatoyo
F Morozumi Masakiyo
G Hara Masatane
H Takeda Nobukado
I Takeda Yoshinobu
J Mochizuki Masayori
K Atobe Katsusuke
L Imafuku Zenkuro
M Asari Nobutane

Saijosan 'woodpecker' force
N Kosaka Danjo Masanobu
O Obu Toramasa (brother of Yamagata)
P Baba Nobuharu
Q Oyamada Bitchu-no-kami Masayuki
R Amari Masatada (son of Torayasu killed at Uedahara)
S Sanada Yukitaka

83

The name in the cartouche reads Yamamoto Kansuke, even though the scene is of Kenshin's attack. The Takeda *mon* (badge) appears on the overturned shield.

what, if anything, was taking place in the Uesugi camp. Also, had Amakasu Kagemochi and his rearguard managed to hold back Kosaka Danjo's force at Amenomiya, Kenshin might well have gained that which he had sought for so long – the head of Takeda Shingen. Instead he failed, but only after Yamamoto Kansuke had paid the ultimate price for his apparent failure of the Takeda.

One remarkable feature of the fourth battle of Kawanakajima is that both commanders claimed it as a victory, although perhaps this is not so surprising when honours were so even. We see this in the text of the kanjo (letter of commendation) from Uesugi Kenshin to Nakajo Fujisuke praising him for his conduct at the battle. Similar ones went to Matsumoto Kageshige, Irobe Katsunaga, Yasuda Nagahide and Suibara Katsuie. The Nakajo version is dated Eiroku 4, 9m 13d (21 October 1561):

> *We departed on the tenth day of the ninth month, and at the time when we gave battle to Takeda Harunobu at Kawanakajima in Shinano, he was a man unparalleled in the earnestness of his efforts. It is a fact that relatives, retainers and even reserve troops, a large number of whom were killed in the battle, were inspired to loyal military service. Even though the rebels sent a thousand horsemen into the attack we won a great victory, an event that will give us great satisfaction for many years to come. Furthermore, there was also much glory gained. The descendants of Uesugi Kagetora will never forget these loyal exploits. We admire his military exploits all the more when set beside the great importance of his loyalty, which is unsurpassed by anyone.*

Uesugi Kenshin's dragon banner always led a charge by his samurai. This reproduction flies proudly at Hachimanbara.

THE FIFTH BATTLE OF KAWANAKAJIMA, 1564

Nothing illustrates the indecisive nature of the bloody fourth battle of Kawanakajima better than the fact that there was a final fifth round in 1564, although it is very much an anticlimax.

In the intervening years Shingen and Kenshin continued their confrontation by assisting allies in neighbouring provinces against each other in a similar fashion to 1557–61. To give but one example, Takeda troops were to be found fighting Uesugi troops at the siege of Matsuyama castle in Musashi province in 1563. Musashi-Matsuyama castle was held by Uesugi Norikatsu and was besieged by an allied army of Hojo Ujiyasu and Takeda Shingen. The latter made good use of miners from Kai who burrowed into the hill on which the castle was built.

In 1564 Takeda Shingen persuaded the Ashina family of Mutsu province to invade Echigo during Kenshin's absence on campaign. Shingen's plan was that the attack would be co-ordinated with an assault he would make into Echigo from Shinano. So on 18 May 1564 local Shinano supporters of the Takeda captured Warigadake castle beside Lake Nojiri. The commander and all his men were killed. With this border fortress as a base Echigo was raided and many villages were burned. The victors were expecting to make contact with the Ashina for a pincer attack on Kasugayama, but when the Uesugi repulsed the Ashina troops the remaining soldiers on the provincial border prudently pulled back. Uesugi samurai then hit back against Shingen and soon recaptured Warigadake. Shingen's raid into Echigo had therefore been a failure, but Kenshin had no way of knowing if the operation was over or if it was merely the preliminary move in another campaign similar to the one that had taken place in 1557. Kenshin therefore responded to Shingen's troublemaking by advancing to Zenkoji on 4 September.

He must have arrived within two days, because on 6 September at a nearby Hachiman shrine, Uesugi Kenshin offered up a prayer for victory. The text has been preserved. It consists largely of a catalogue of Takeda Shingen's misdeeds, beginning with the forced exile of his father. Kenshin lists seven categories of Takeda wrongdoing including several failures of a religious nature. Shingen, he states, had been remiss in overseeing religious ceremonies and had assigned secular authorities to supervise temples and shrines when he invaded Shinano:

Now that Shingen has destroyed Shinano's temples and shrines and exiled their priests, who could possibly respect the authority of the kami if they allow him to continue gaining victories?

This was strong stuff, and it was Kenshin himself who was destined to be the instrument of punishment, avenging the names of Ogasawara, Murakami, Takanashi and all the others who had suffered over the past three decades from Takeda Shingen's expansionist policies.

On 8 September Kenshin crossed the Saigawa and entered the Kawanakajima plain in battle array against the Takeda for what was to prove the last time. But Shingen showed no signs of advancing to meet him, so there was no immediate prospect of the decisive battle that

Kenshin had promised. On 9 September Kenshin wrote a letter to Satake Yoshinobu of Hitachi province in which he expresses his frustration at Shingen's absence. He also confirmed his intentions to make Saku into Uesugi territory.

It was the beginning of October before Takeda Shingen finally obliged his rival by advancing to Kawanakajima and establishing a field position. He approached by a different route from before, using the passes up from Fukashi (Matsumoto). This helped determine his choice of battle location, which this time was the hill of Shiozaki. It lay across the Chikumagawa south of Chausuyama, and was the furthest west of the positions selected in any of the battles. It was a very clever move, because Shingen had occupied the higher ground, and by advancing from Matsumoto he had cleverly trapped Kenshin between Shiozaki and Kaizu.

The battle of Shiozaki, October 1564

The standoff at Shiozaki was destined to be almost the sum total of the fifth battle of Kawanakajima, because there was little fighting over the next few days. Instead of the major clash that Kenshin still desired both sides replayed the futile scenario of the second battle. Kenshin understood the hopelessness of his position and had no desire to be reckless. An advance upstream to Saku was now out of the question. By using the minimum of force Shingen had very neatly demonstrated that the Kawanakajima area was Takeda property and that Uesugi Kenshin was now sitting in enemy territory. Kenshin had little choice but to withdraw, and Shingen let him go.

Uesugi Kenshin rallied his troops and pulled them back to Iiyama castle, his nearest safe haven on the border. Without a moment's delay the Takeda army advanced after them, but not to engage them in battle. Instead Shingen sent soldiers into the now abandoned Motodoriyama castle that guarded the site of the third battle of Kawanakajima and took down the Uesugi flags. He then crossed the Chikumagawa to the eastern bank and advanced to his safe haven of Takanashi. In response Kenshin ordered repairs to Iiyama castle, strengthened its defences, and then on 4 November he returned to Kasugayama.

The 1564 challenge, otherwise known as the fifth battle of Kawanakajima, seemed to have drawn a line between Shingen and Kenshin. The armed standoff had been in effect an unspoken peace conference where both delegates had made their feelings clear by actions rather than words. The anticlimactic finish to the fifth battle of Kawanakajima also marked the end of Uesugi Kenshin's battle-seeking obsession and set the limits of each other's spheres of influence among the high peaks on the Echigo/Shinano border. Uesugi Kenshin was never again to descend with an army from those mountains on to the flatlands beyond. The final battle of Kawanakajima had been fought.

AFTERMATH

In the years that followed the last battle of Kawanakajima the rivalry and mistrust between Shingen and Kenshin ensured that the war continued by other means. In 1565 Kenshin revealed in a letter of 19 August to a castle commander in Kozuke province that he still wished to invade Shinano to liberate the province, but that 'times had changed'. Fighting between them now went on in neighbouring provinces as each assisted his enemy's enemies.

The siege of Minowa in 1566 is one outstanding example of this policy. Minowa castle in Kozuke was defended fiercely by a strong retainer of the Uesugi called Nagano Narimasa. For this reason Takeda Shingen had left it well alone, but when Narimasa died, fearful lest the Takeda should take advantage of this the Nagano followers kept his death secret for as long as possible while his heir Narimori consolidated his position.

The Takeda soon realised what had happened and launched their attack in 1566. The great swordsman Kamiizumi Hidetsuna took part in the defence of Minowa with the young heir leading at the front. Attack after attack was repulsed, with the action characterised almost exclusively by hand-to-hand combat, helped by some ingenious defence works that included piles of logs released beside the gate when an attack took place. Finally Hidetsuna took the fight to the Takeda and sallied

Another scene from the re-enactment of Uesugi Kenshin's departure for war at Yonezawa. Here the actor playing Kenshin is shown in a vivid white headcowl as he makes an offering at a Shinto shrine.

out of the castle in a bold surge. The Takeda became demoralised, but then fate took a hand, for in another sally by the defenders the young heir Narimori was cut down and killed, and this time there was no opportunity to keep a commander's death secret. The Takeda seized upon this huge psychological weapon, and the shattered defenders were forced to sue for peace.

The 'sixth battle' of Kawanakajima, The Shinano/Echigo border, 3 August 1568

In 1568 the mountains and valleys on the border area between Echigo and Shinano were to echo to the sound of fighting for one last time. With Kawanakajima now firmly established as a Takeda island, the Uesugi sphere of influence in Shinano was confined to its northern tip. In 1567 the Ichikawa family, based north of Iiyama castle, declared for Shingen, and Shingen gave orders for the restoration of Nagahama castle on the border. This former Shimazu possession received extensive repairs and a castle town was created around it. Nagahama now provided a rival to Kenshin's Iiyama.

After this, Shingen devised a complex scheme. In 1568 he worked on the daimyo of Etchu province to unite against Kenshin. Kenshin retaliated by invading Etchu, but while he was absent Shingen won over to his side Kenshin's renowned general Honjo Shigenaga. Takeda Shingen judged that the time was ripe to take advantage of Kenshin's problems and invade Echigo. Even if he could not reach Kasugayama, merely to wipe off the map Iiyama and the other border outposts would bring his long Shinano campaign to a successful conclusion after 26 years.

So Shingen led an army to Kawanakajima for the last time. He advanced to his secure and trusty base of Kaizu castle, from where on 3 August 1568 he sent a detachment forward to attack Iiyama. While they were on their way along the Chikumagawa route Shingen led his main body even further into the Togakushi/Iizuna than he had dared go during the glory days of 1553–64. From Togakushi he entered his new outpost of Nagahama castle, from where he could easily invade Echigo.

Kenshin responded immediately to the twin threats by sending reinforcements to Iiyama castle and to his newly built fortress of Sekida on

The death of Takeda Shingen at Noda in 1573. He was shot by a sniper from the walls of the castle.

the pass of the same name that had provided his means of entry into Shinano on so many previous occasions. In this Uesugi Kenshin displayed great determination and a sensible order of precedence. He was not so preoccupied with resisting rebels in his own province that he would neglect an invasion from Shinano by Takeda Shingen.

The stage was set for another Uesugi advance down into the plains of northern Shinano and perhaps even a sixth battle of Kawanakajima. Times had changed for both protagonists, however, and the armies stayed on the border. There may not have been a sixth battle and the two commanders may not actually have been in Kawanakajima, but the stalemate that ensued with Takeda Shingen glaring down from Nagahama and Uesugi Kenshin glaring back at him from Iiyama differed only from the 1555 and 1564 scenarios in its precise location.

For Shingen it had been enough just to threaten Kenshin with an invasion. He was now almost literally sitting on the Echigo border, the monarch of all he surveyed in a southerly direction. He probably had no intention of attacking Kasugayama castle. Instead he had drawn a line in the snow to remind his rival of where they stood. After 26 years Shinano was his.

Kenshin too managed to satisfy himself with the inevitable situation. His border was secure, and he had long since given up his obsessive goal of seeking a final pitched battle with Shingen. Times had indeed changed, and both rivals knew that events occurring far off in the west were to alter the balance of power in Japan forever, and make the long Takeda/Uesugi rivalry seem a matter of little consequence. While Shingen and Kenshin were conducting their last eyeball-to-eyeball confrontation on the Shinano/Echigo border the up-and-coming daimyo Oda Nobunaga succeeded where every other daimyo since the Onin War had failed. He marched on Kyoto, secured the capital and set up his own nominee, Ashikaga Yoshiaki, as Shogun.

For Takeda Shingen in particular this meant a radical rethinking of his strategic position. No longer was it imperative upon him to head north towards the Sea of Japan. That part of the country was now an irrelevant backwater that could be left to Kenshin. The real seat of activity had shifted to the Pacific coast, from which landlocked Kai was separated by the territories of the mighty Hojo and another young daimyo allied to Oda Nobunaga called Tokugawa Ieyasu. Thus it was that Takeda Shingen's new policy saw him heading south in 1569 for an unsuccessful siege of the Hojo's Odawara castle. It was a dismal failure, and to add insult to injury the Hojo samurai ambushed him at the battle of Mimasetoge (Mimase Pass) on his return.

The battle of Mikata ga Hara and the siege of Noda, 1572–73

Takeda Shingen had much more success when he turned his attentions towards Tokugawa territory. At Mikata ga Hara in 1572 he won a cavalry victory in classic Takeda style but failed to consolidate his triumph by capturing Hamamatsu castle. He renewed his attempts to destroy Tokugawa Ieyasu when the snows melted the following year. The Takeda laid siege to Ieyasu's castle of Noda in Mikawa province and were very successful, so the garrison prepared for a honourable surrender. According to an enduring legend the defenders, knowing that their end was near, decided to dispose of their stocks of sake (rice wine) in the most appropriate manner. The Takeda samurai in the besieging camp could hear the noise of their drunken celebrations and took note of one Tokugawa samurai who was playing a flute rather well. Takeda Shingen approached the ramparts to hear the tune, and a vigilant guard, who was less drunk than his companions, took an arquebus and put a bullet through the great daimyo's head. The death of their beloved leader was kept secret for as long as the Takeda could manage, but the news eventually leaked out.

The death of Yamamoto Kansuke at Kawanakajima. Although handicapped by having only one good leg and one good eye, Yamamoto Kansuke had risen to be Shingen's right-hand man and was nearly 70 years old at Kawanakajima. He accepted full responsibility for the disaster that his error of judgement had brought upon them, and resolved to make amends by dying like a true samurai.

Takeda Yoshinobu, who had fought so bravely at Kawanakajima, had died young in 1567, so Shingen was succeeded by his able but headstrong son Takeda Katsuyori. He was the son of the lady of Suwa whom Shingen had seized in one of his earliest incursions into Shinano province. To many people she had brought a curse on the family, and their doom would be accomplished through the son she had born to Shingen. This prophecy was to come true all too soon in 1575 on the battlefield of Nagashino. Katsuyori's defeat marked the end of the Takeda as a military force of any consequence in central Japan. The clan lingered on for seven more years, but never again would a Takeda army leave Kai to bring war to its neighbours.

The fall of the Uesugi, 1578

As for Uesugi Kenshin, still the nominal 'lord of the Kanto', he battled on against the Hojo on one side and Oda Nobunaga on the other. In fact Kenshin inflicted upon Oda Nobunaga one of the few defeats of his career. This was the night battle of Tedorigawa in 1577, a considerable victory gained by using a manoeuvre that had echoes of Kenshin's crossing of the Chikumagawa at Amenomiya at the fourth battle of Kawanakajima in 1561.

Kenshin now looked destined to be one of the few daimyo who would have the resources and the skills to oppose the seemingly irresistible rise of Oda Nobunaga. But a year later a servant heard cries from inside Kenshin's lavatory and found his lord dying and unable to speak. He had probably had a stroke, but his death was so fortuitous for Oda Nobunaga that ninja were suspected. On his death the Uesugi domains were divided between his heir Kagetora, the son of Hojo Ujiyasu whom the celibate Kenshin had adopted, and his nephew Kagekatsu, son of his brother-in-law Nagao Masakage.

The rivals of the Uesugi were already gathering like vultures, and in a scenario that could not have been any more favourable to their enemies the two cousins went to war with each other. Within a short space of time

Uesugi Kagetora was dead. Kagekatsu was now the undisputed lord of the Uesugi, but their power had been broken forever.

Kawanakajima – from battle to myth

By the early 1580s, when the territories of Takeda and Uesugi had ceased to mean anything in the context of Japanese politics, the Kawanakajima area became a backwater in more ways than one. Ueda, the town just to the south of the battlefield, became the seat of the Sanada family, who were descended from one of Shingen's Twenty-Four Generals. It grew in importance because it lay on the Nakasendo road. This was one of the two main highways between Kyoto and Edo, the city now called Tokyo that became the capital of the Tokugawa family, who had destroyed the Takeda in 1582.

During the Tokugawa Period, Kawanakajima as battlefield gave way to Kawanakajima as myth. The five battles became a popular topic for woodblock printmakers during the 19th century and depictions of Shingen and Kenshin sold in their thousands. Because both families had died out there was no danger of embarrassing the Tokugawa government, so the censors left pictures of Kawanakajima alone. As for the site of the great encounters, the plain was farmed and yielded much fruit. So remote was the area that Matsumoto castle (the former Fukashi) was fortunately spared the loyal and modernising demolition mania that afflicted so much of Japan in the late 19th century and remains to this day the oldest extant tower keep in arguably the most beautiful castle in Japan.

Following the Meiji Restoration, Shinano province became Nagano Prefecture. Not many years later the mountains beyond Matsumoto that had provided the backdrop to the Kawanakajima campaigns were 'discovered' by an English missionary called Walter Weston. He christened them the 'Japan Alps' and introduced the modern concept of mountaineering to Japan. While Victorian enthusiasts hiked along the paths once trodden by Shingen's raiders the great Zenkoji temple continued to display the exact copy of Japan's first Buddhist statue every seven years. Meanwhile the city of Nagano gradually spread around it. Both the Susohanagawa and Chikumagawa changed their courses, while down on the plain modern roads and railways began to cut their way across what had once been the site of five battles. A century later the cross-country skiers of the 1998 Winter Olympics raced each other through the passes that had echoed to the Takeda/Uesugi border wars. Only the Saigawa stayed roughly where it had been all those centuries ago, still creating with the help of the Chikumagawa a curious triangular island between them that would always bear the stirring name of Kawanakajima.

THE BATTLEFIELD TODAY

Kawanakajima is one of the most evocative of all the 16th-century Japanese battlefields. The best starting point is Nagano City. If you have arrived at Nagano from either Tokyo or Nagoya you will have already crossed the battlefield by train. Take a bus (20 minutes) for Matsushiro, and alight at Kawanakajima. The bus stop is next to Hachimanbara and its splendid statues of the single-combat beside a simple Shinto shrine among the trees. As well as the site itself there is a modern museum that has a very good audio-visual show in Japanese about the fourth battle of Kawanakajima. The grave of Morozumi Masakiyo is to the north, on the way back to Nagano.

To complete the tour walk half a mile down to the Chikumagawa River and see Nobushige's grave in the temple called the Tenkyuji, which is on the right just before the modern bridge. The main hall of the temple houses a renowned image of Emma-do, the guardian of hell. There is a very interesting little museum, which contains, among other items, one of Shingen's helmets. Yamamoto Kansuke's grave may be seen by crossing the bridge. Then take the bus again or walk into the pleasant town of Matsushiro and see the ruins of Kaizu Castle and a number of historic buildings associated with the Sanada family. The more energetic may then climb Saijosan for the panoramic view from Kenshin's camp.

Northwest of Nagano lie the anonymous-looking hills on which the castles of Asahiyama and Katsurayama once stood. The Togakushi area is very interesting and has many other historical associations with the site of the cave where Amaterasu the Sun Goddess hid. This is now marked by a series of shrines, and there is a ninja museum in the vicinity. Across

Takeda Shingen holds court at his mansion of Tsutsugasaki. Several portraits of Shingen survive show a consistently strong image. He was a solidly built, determined-looking man, portrayed in later life with elaborate side-whiskers.

The Chikumagawa looking towards the southwest and the site of the ford of Amenomiya, where Kenshin crossed the river on his way to and from Saijosan.

Another scene from the 2001 re-enactment of Takeda Shingen's departure for war at Kofu. The banners display the Mon badges of various Takeda retainers.

the Chikumagawa valley from Motodoriyama is the world-famous spa of Shiga Kogen where the wild monkeys come down to share the baths with humans!

Re-enactment events

Strange to relate, the main re-enactment events designed to celebrate the battles of Kawanakajima take place nowhere near Nagano. Instead one must journey to Yonezawa in Yamagata Prefecture, the castle town that became the Uesugi fief after the fall of Uesugi Kagekatsu, to see the 'Uesugi Butei Shiki' – the ceremony of Uesugi Kenshin departing for war. In recent years this has included a battle re-enactment as well. Yonezawa also has a very lively society of arquebus enthusiasts, who may be seen firing their weapons at various festivals around the country.

Not to be outdone, Kofu, Takeda Shingen's capital, has its own spectacular Takeda departure re-enactment as part of its annual spring festival every April. At nearby Isawa, which has a convenient dried-up riverbed not unlike the Saigawa, there is a large-scale annual re-enactment of the battle of Kawanakajima with thousands of enthusiastic participants. Details of all these events may be found through the Japan Tourist Organisation, which has branches in major capital cities.

FURTHER READING

There are precious few written records for any of these battles except for the fourth, and even for this our main source is the epic called *Koyo Gunkan*, a chronicle of the Takeda family, whose authorship is attributed to Kosaka Danjo Masanobu, one of Takeda Shingen's lifelong retainers and a veteran of at least one of the five battles. *Koyo Gunkan* is supposed to have been written soon after the event. It is in epic style, and fits with other descriptions, with oral tradition, and with local topography. *Koyo Gunkan* has never been translated into English in its entirety, although small sections from it appear in various English-language works. A useful Japanese edition appears in *Sengoku Shiryo Sosho Series 1* Volumes 3–5 (1965), which I have used for my own translations which appear here.

The best secondary work in Japanese on the campaigns is *Kawanakajima no tatakai* by Keichiro Kobayashi (1985). There is also a very good illustrated booklet published by the battlefield museum also called *Kawanakajima no tatakai*. It is on sale at Hachimanbara. There is also a wealth of detail about Takeda Shingen and Uesugi Kenshin in several volumes of Gakken's *Rekishi Gunzo* Series, particularly Volume 5, *Takeda Shingen*; Volume 6, *Furin Kazan*; Volume 7, *Sanada Gunki*; and Volume 8, *Uesugi Kenshin*.

For the heraldry of the Takeda Twenty-Four Generals, and background details about Shingen and Kenshin, see my *Samurai: The Warrior Tradition* (Cassells 1996) or the older *Samurai Warlords: the book of the daimyo* (Cassells 1989), which contains exactly the same material. For a guide to samurai warfare see my *Samurai Warfare* (Cassells 1996) and *The Samurai Sourcebook* (Cassells 1998). The tragic story of the Takeda clan continues in Osprey Campaigns Series 69 *Nagashino 1575* (Osprey 2000).

I would also recommend any reader to view the film *Samurai Banners*, a subtitled version of the original *Furin Kazan* ('Wind, forest, fire and mountain') from the characters on Shingen's banners. It tells the story of Yamamoto Kansuke and finishes with the fourth battle of Kawanakajima. The battle sequences of Uedahara and Kawanakajima are very well done. It is readily available in a video format.

INDEX

Figures in **bold** refer to illustrations

Amakasu Kagemochi 65, 74, 77, **78–9**, 81, 84
Amakazari castle 61
Amari Torayasu 30
Amaterasu o mikami (Sun Goddess) 49, 92
Amenomiya 61–2, 64, 73, 74, 77, 84, **92**
Anayama Nobukimi 68, 76
Ankokuji castle 28
Arakawa 76
Arato castle 42
arquebuses 24
Asahiyama castle 8, **34**, 35, **39**, 45, 46, **48**, 54, 55, 92
Asari Nobutane 68
ashigaru 23–4
ashigaru taisho 21
Ashikaga family 9, 13
Ashikaga Yoshiaki 89
Ashina family 60, 85
atenori (cavalry charge) 23
Atobe Katsusuke 68

Baba Nobuharu 32, 40, 48, **49**, **50–1**, **78–9**
battle formations **24**, **45**, 68, 75

Chausuyama 62
Chikumagawa River **9**, **20**, 26, 34, 39, 42, 44, 61, **78–9**, 91, 92, **92**
Chino Yugeinojo 48

Daihoji family 60
Daimon Pass 26, 30, 40
daimyo (great names) 9, 11
do maru (armour) **55**

Echigo 8, 11, 33, 36, 85, 88
Etchu 88

firearms 23–4, 31
Fuchu 13, 16
fudai (inner retainers) 22
Fudo **16**
Fuji River 11
Fujiwara family 16
Fujizawa Yorichika 28
Fukashi (later Matsumoto) castle 23, 31, 40, 86, 91
Fukuyo castle 28
Furin Kazan (film) 30, **56**
Fuse, battle of (1553) 7, 8, 37, 41, **41**

Gempei War (1180–85) 9, 13
go fudai karo-shu 21
Go gunyaku cho 22
goshinrui-shu 21
Gyorin (battle formation) **24**

Hachiman, battles of (1553) 8, 35–6, 37, 39, **39**, **40**, 42
Hachimanbara 7, 8, 57, **63**, 64, **70–1**, 84
head mound **88**
single combat at **74**, 75–6, **76**, **77**
today 92
Hajikano Den'emon 30
Hamamatsu castle 90
Hara Masatane 68
Hara Osumi-no-kami 75–6
haramaki armour **55**
hatamoto shoyakunin 21
Himeji castle 23
Hiraga Genshin 14
hirajiro (castle) 61
hirotachi no shu 22
Hojo family 11, 13, 17, 60, 89, 90
Hojo Tsunanari 17
Hojo Ujiyasu 17, 19, 60, 85, 90
Honda Yoshimitsu 44
Honjo Saneyori 17
Honjo Shigenaga 22, 88
Hosokawa Yoriharu 24–5

Ichikawa family 88
Ichikawa Fujiyoshi 56
Iiyama castle 34, 49, 86, 88
siege of (1557) 53–6
Iizuna 47, 48
Ikko-ikki 16
Imafuku Zenkuro 68
Imagawa family 11
Imagawa Yoshimoto 15, 57
Irobe Katsunaga 49, 76, 84
Isawa 93
Ishiguro Goro 77
Itagaki Nobukata 28, 30, 63
Itoigawa valley 42–3
Iwahana 55

Japan, central **10**
'Japan Alps' 91
jikishindan 21
jikitachi no shu 22
jinbaori (surcoat) **15**, **24**
Joshoji temple 48
Joyama 44, 45

Kai 11, 13, 15, 26
Kaizu castle 61, **61**, 62, 63
Kakizaki Kageie 65, **68**, **70–1**, 74, 76
kakuyoku (battle formation) 68
Kamiizumi Hidetsuna 87–8
Kanai Hidekage 30
Kanto 11, 17, 60
Kasahara Kiyoshige 29–30
Kasugayama castle 17, 18, 34, **53**, 60, 86, 89
Katsurao castle 30, 33, 35, 40

Katsurayama castle **34**, 42
siege of (1557) 8, 47–9, **50–1**
site **48**, 92
Kawagoe castle 17
Kawanakajima
battlefield today **9**, 92–3
re-enactments 93
romance of 7
topography 34–5
Kawanakajima, 1st battle of (1553) 37, **38**, 39–42
Kawanakajima, 2nd battle of (1555) 24, **41**, 42–7, **43**, **46**
Kawanakajima, 3rd battle of (1557) 47–9, 53–7, **54**
Kawanakajima, 4th battle of (1561)
casualties 81
Kenshin's dawn attack 73–5
Kosaka Danjo's counterattack 77
numbers involved 64–5, 68
Operation Woodpecker 63–4, 68–9, 73, **78–9**, 81
single combat at **74**, 75–6, **76**, **77**
site **63**, 81, 84
Takeda Shingen's advance to 62–3
Kawanakajima, 5th battle of (1564) 85–6
Kawanakajima, '6th battle of' (1568) 88–9
kesa (scarf) **6**
kiba gundan (mounted warband) 23
Kiso Yoshiyasu 26, 42
Kofu 93
Kojima Yataro 20, 76, **77**
Kojinyama 28, 29
Komai Masatake 28
Kosaka castle 55
Kosaka Danjo Masanobu 15, 62, 64, 73, 77, **78–9**, 84
Koyo Gunkan (chronicle) 15, 20, 21, 30, 31, 62, 63, 64, 68, 69, 72, 75
Kozuke 60
kuni-shu 21
Kurita Kakuju 45
Kuroda Hidetada 17
Kurotaki castle 17
kuruma gakari (battle formation) 75
Kuwabara castle 26, 28
Kyoto 9, 89

Matsumoto (formerly Fukashi) castle 23, 31, 40, 86, 91
Matsumoto Kageshige **70–1**, 84
Matsushiro **63**, 84, 92
Matsuyama, siege of (1563) 85
Meiji Restoration 91
Mikata ga Hara, battle of (1572) 23, 89–90
Mimasetoge, battle of (1569) 89
Minamoto family 9
Minamoto Yoritomo 13

Minamoto Yoshiie 13
Minamoto Yoshikiyo 13
Minamoto Yoshimitsu 13
Minowa, siege of (1566) 87–8
Mochizuki Masayori 68
Morozumi Masakiyo 68, **70–1**, 74, 77, 92
   death 76, **81**
Motodoriyama castle 42, 49, 53, 55, 56, 86, 93
Mount Fuji 11, **13**, **15**
Murakami Yoshikiyo 19, 20, 26, 30, 31, 32, 33, 36, 39, 40, 85
Myohoji-ki (chronicle) 30

nagaeyari (spear) 24
Nagahama castle 49, 88, 89
Nagakubo castle 29
Nagano **9**, 42, 91, 92
Nagano Narimasa 87
Nagano Narimori 87, 88
Nagao family 11
Nagao Harukage 16–17
Nagao Kageyasu 16, 17
Nagao Masakage 53, 60, 65, 90
Nagao Tamekage 16
Nagashino, battle of (1575) 29, 36, 90
naginata (spear) **11**, 24
Naito Masatoyo **49**, 68, **70–1**, 74
Nakajo Fujisuke 22, 76, 84
Naoe Kagetsuna 65, 74, 81
Nirasaki, battle of (1541) 15
Noda, siege of (1573) 90
nodowa (throat guard) **55**
Nojiri, Lake 49, 85
norikiri (cavalry charge) 23
norikuzushi (cavalry charge) 23

Obu Toramasa 40, **78–9**
Ochiai Bitchu no kami 48, **50–1**
Oda Nobunaga 57, 89, 90
Odaihara, battle of (1546) 30
Odawara castle 60, 89
Ogasawara Nagatoki 26, 31–2, 85
Ogigayatsu Uesugi family 16, 17
Ohashi Yajiro 56
Oi Sadakiyo 29
Oi Sadataka 29
Okehazama, battle of (1560) 57
Omi 42
On tachi no shidai 22
Onin War 9, 13
Oso Gempachiro 40
o-sode (shoulder guards) **55**
Otari castle 55
Otsuka 45, 61
Oyamada Nobushige 32

Rai San'yo 14, 19, 32–3, 73
ronin 21
Ryugasaki castle 29

Saigawa River 7, 8, 26, 34, **41**, 42, **44**, 45–7, **46**, 91
Saijosan hill **41**, **60**, 62, 63, 64, 73, 77, 81, **81**, 92
Saito Tomonobu 60, 65
Sakaki 42, 55
sakikata-shu 21
Saku campaign 29–30

Saku valley 26, 55, 86
Sambonji Sadanaga 60, 65
samurai
   armour **55**
   in battle **19**
   mounted **11**, 21, 22–3, **23**
samurai-shu 22
Sanada family 21, 91
Sanada Yukitaka 33, 61
Sasama 68
sashimono **47**
Satake Yoshinobu 86
Sekida castle 88–9
Sendanno, battle of (1536) 16
Sengoku Period 8–9, 11
'Seventeen Generals' 20
Sezawa, battle of (1542) 26, 28
Shibata Harunaga 76
Shiga castle, siege of (1547) 29–30
Shiga Kogen spa 93
Shimazu family 49, 88
Shimodaira Yashichiro 56
Shinano 11
   Takeda Shingen's conquest of (1536–68) 8, 26–33, **27**
Shioda castle, siege of (1553) 40–2
Shiojiritoge, battle of (1548) 32
Shiozaki 7
   battle of (1564) 86
shogunate 9, 89
signalling beacons **62**
Suda Chikamitsu **70–1**
Suibara Katsuie **70–1**, 84
Suruga 15
Susohanagawa River 34, **34**, 35, **37**, 42, 91
Suwa campaign (1542) 26, 28–9
Suwa Yorishige 26, 28

Taiheiki 24–5
Taira family 13
Takanashi castle 61
Takanashi Masayori 53, 55, 85
Takashima 40
Takato castle 29
Takato Yoritsugu 28, 29, 31, 42
Takeda Katsuyori 29, 90
Takeda Nobukado 68
Takeda Nobushige
   at 4th battle 65, 68, 74, 77, **77**
   grave **69**, 92
   at Katsurao 33
Takeda Nobutora 13–14, 15, 26
Takeda Nobuyoshi 13
Takeda Shingen **6**, **14**, **15**, **24**, **28**, **46** **75**, **77**
   army 20–1
   command structure 20, 65
   death **89**, 90
   departure ceremony **22**, **29**, **31**, **93**, **93**
   at Mikata ga Hara (1572) 89–90
   at Nirasaki (1541) 15
   personal life 15–16
   plans 36
   rise to power 13–15
   Saku campaign 29–30
   Shinano, conquest of (1536–68) 8, 26–33, **27**
   single combat at Hachimanbara **74**, 75–6, **76**, **77**

'Son Zi' flag **24**, **48**
Suwa campaign 26, 28–9
   at Toishi (1550) 32–3
   at Uedahara (1548) 30–1
   at Umi no kuchi (1536) 14
   yashiki (mansion) 16, **17**, **92**
   see also Kawanakajima, battles of
Takeda Yoshinobu 33, 68, 75, 90
Takemata Hirotsuna **70–1**, 74
tanto (dagger) 25
Tedorigawa, battle of (1577) 90
Tenkyuji temple 92
Tochio castle 17
Togakushi mountains 35, **35**, 47, 49, 92
Toishi castle 32–3
Toksan, siege of (1593) 49
Tokugawa Ieyasu 16, 89, 90
Toshiro Mifune **56**
tozama (outer retainers) 22
Tsutsujigasaki 16, **17**, 23, 62, **92**
'Twenty-Four Generals' 20, 21, **21**, **49**
'Twenty-Eight Generals' 20, 76

Uchiyama 29, 32
Ueda 91
Uedahara, battle of (1548) 23, 23–4, 30–1
Uehara castle 26, 28
Uenohara 7, 8, 55
   battle of (1557) 56–7
Uesugi family 16
Uesugi Kagekatsu 90, 93
Uesugi Kagetora 90–1
Uesugi Kenshin 8, **18**, **26**, **41**, **47**, **75**
   army 22
   command structure 20, 65, 68
   death 90
   departure ceremony 35, **87**, 93
   dragon banner **85**
   personal life 19
   plans 35–6
   rise to power 16–17
   single combat at Hachimanbara **74**, 75–6, **76**, **77** *see also* Kawanakajima, battles of
Uesugi Norikatsu 85
Uesugi Norimasa 17, 30
Uesugi Sadazane 17
Uji, battles of (1180–1221) 7
Umi no kuchi, siege of (1536) 14, 26
Usami Sadayuki 81

Wada 40
Warigadake castle 34, 60, 85
Weston, Walter 91

Yamagata Masakage 55, 56, 68, 76, 77
Yamamoto Kansuke Haruyuki 32–3, **56**, 63, **64**, 68, 76, 77, **78–9**, 84, **84**, **90**, 92
Yamanouchi Uesugi family 16, 17
yamashiro (mountain castles) 11, **50–1**, **53**
   warfare 23
yari (spear) 24–5
Yasuda Nagahide 84
Yokata Takatoshi 32
Yonezawa 93

Zenkoji temple 35, **35**, 42, 43–5, **44**, 54, 55, 61, 74, 91

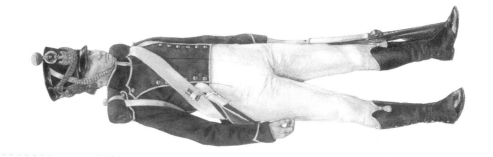

FIND OUT MORE ABOUT OSPREY

❏ Please send me the latest listing of Osprey's publications

❏ I would like to subscribe to Osprey's e-mail newsletter

Title / rank

Name

Address

City / county

Postcode / zip   state / country

e-mail

I am interested in:

❏ Ancient world   ❏ American Civil War
❏ Medieval world   ❏ World War 1
❏ 16th century   ❏ World War 2
❏ 17th century   ❏ Modern warfare
❏ 18th century   ❏ Military aviation
❏ Napoleonic   ❏ Naval warfare
❏ 19th century

Please send to:

USA & Canada:
Osprey Direct USA, c/o MBI Publishing, P.O. Box 1,
729 Prospect Avenue, Osceola, WI 54020

UK, Europe and rest of world:
Osprey Direct UK, P.O. Box 140, Wellingborough,
Northants, NN8 2FA, United Kingdom

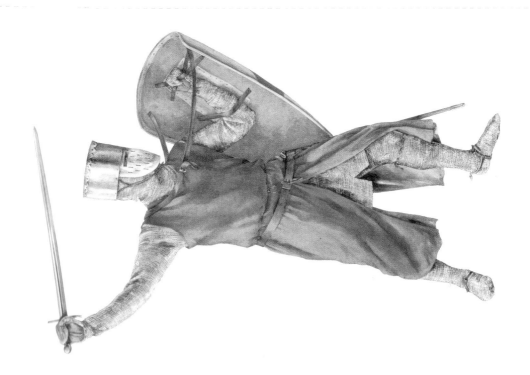

www.ospreypublishing.com

call our telephone hotline
for a free information pack

USA & Canada: 1-800-826-6600
UK, Europe and rest of world call:
+44 (0) 1933 443 863

Young Guardsman
Figure taken from *Warrior 22:*
Imperial Guardsman 1799–1815
Published by Osprey
Illustrated by Christa Hook

Knight, c.1190
Figure taken from *Warrior 1: Norman Knight 950 – 1204 AD*
Published by Osprey
Illustrated by Christa Hook

POSTCARD

DR